DIALOGUES

BOLLINGEN SERIES XLV

The Collected Works of Paul Valéry

Edited by Jackson Mathews

VOLUME 4

PAUL VALÉRY

DIALOGUES

Translated by
William McCausland Stewart

With Two Prefaces by
Wallace Stevens

BOLLINGEN SERIES XLV · 4

PRINCETON UNIVERSITY PRESS

THIS IS VOLUME FOUR OF THE
COLLECTED WORKS OF PAUL VALÉRY
CONSTITUTING NUMBER XLV IN THE BOLLINGEN SERIES.

Library of Congress catalog card no. 56-9337
ISBN 0-691-01878-2
Text designed by Andor Braun
Cover designed by Margaret Davis
Cover illustration: Portrait of Valery
by D'Espagnat, from the
Giraudon "Célébrités françaises" Collection,
reproduced with the permission of
Art Resource, New York.
Printed in the United States of America

CONTENTS

TWO PREFACES

by

Wallace Stevens

Gloire du long Désir, Idées

DENIS SAURAT refers to *Eupalinos* as Valéry's "prose master-piece," not meaning more, however, than that it was one of a number of masterpieces by Valéry in prose, not to speak of his masterpieces in verse. He cites a brief passage or two and then says, "You have to go back to Bossuet to find such writing in prose." It is easy to believe this of *Eupalinos* if you give yourself up to some of the more rhetorical episodes. There is, for example, the passage in which Socrates speaks of the chance that had placed in his hands an object which became, for him, the source of reflections on the difference between constructing and knowing. Phaedrus asked him to help him to see the object, and thereupon Socrates said:

Well then, Phaedrus, this is how it was. I was walking on the very edge of the sea. I was following an endless shore. . . . This is not a dream I am telling you. I was going I know not whither, over-flowing with life, half-intoxicated by my youth. The air, deliciously rude and pure, pressing against my face and limbs, confronted me—an impalpable hero that I must vanquish in order to advance. And this resistance, ever overcome, made of me, too, at every step an imaginary hero, victorious over the wind, and rich in energies that were ever reborn, ever equal to the power of the invisible adversary. . . . That is just what youth is. I trod firmly the winding beach, beaten and hardened by the waves. All things around me were simple and pure: the sky, the sand, the water.

Merely to share the balance and the imagery of these words is to share the particular exhilaration of the experience itself. Then, too, toward the close of the work, in the speech in which Socrates states the conclusions to which the speakers have been brought, he substitutes for oral exhilaration the exhilaration that comes from the progression of the mind. Only enough of this true apostrophe can be cited to identify it. Socrates says to Phaedrus:

O coeternal with me in death, faultless friend, and diamond of sincerity, hear then:

It served no purpose, I fear, to seek this God, whom I have tried all my life to discover, by pursuing him through the realm of thought alone; by demanding him of that most variable and most ignoble sense of the just and the unjust, and by urging him to surrender to the solicitings of the most refined dialectic. The God that one so finds is but a word born of words, and returns to the word. For the reply we make to ourselves is assuredly never anything other than the question itself; and every question put by the mind to the mind is only, and can only be, a piece of simplicity. But on the contrary, it is in acts, and in the combination of acts, that we ought to find the most immediate feeling of the presence of the divine, and the best use for that part of our strength that is unnecessary for living, and seems to be reserved for the pursuits of an indefinable object that infinitely transcends us.

Valéry himself has commented on the work. In a letter to Paul Souday written in 1923, he said:

I was asked to write a text for the album *Architectures*, which is a collection of engravings and plans. Since this text was to be magnificently printed in folio format and fitted in exactly with the decoration and pagination of the work, I was requested to limit its size quite précisely to 115,800 *letters* . . . 115,800 characters! It is true, the characters were to be sumptuous.

I accepted. My dialogue was at first too long. I shortened it; and then a little too short—I lengthened it. I came to find these exigencies very interesting, though it is possible that the text itself may have suffered a little in consequence.

After all, the sculptors never complained who were obliged to house their Olympian personages inside the obtuse triangle of pediments! . . .

There is, also, a letter to Dontenville, *inspecteur d'Académie,* written in 1934. The letter to Paul Souday was written a few months after the composition of *Eupalinos.* The letter to Dontenville was written after the lapse of ten years. Valéry, referring again to the requirement of 115,800 characters, said:

This rigor, at first astounding and repellent, albeit required of a man accustomed enough to the rigor of poems in fixed form, made this man wonder at first—but then find that the peculiar condition proposed to him might be easily enough satisfied by employing the very elastic form of the *dialogue.* (An insignificant rejoinder, introduced or cut out, allows us after a few fumblings to conform with fixed requirements of measurement.) The adjustment was, in effect, easily made in the proofs.

The vast proof sheets I received gave me the strange impression that I had in my hands a work of the sixteenth century and was 400 years dead.

The name of Eupalinos was taken by me from the article "Architecture" in the *Encyclopédie Berthelot,* when I was looking for the name of an architect. I since learned, from a study by the learned Hellenist Bidez (of Ghent), that Eupalinos, an engineer more than an architect, dug canals and built scarcely any temples; I gave him my ideas, as I did Socrates and Phaedrus. Moreover, I have never been in Greece; and as for Greek, I have unfortunately remained the most indifferent of scholars, getting lost in the original text of Plato and finding him, in the translations, terribly long and often boring. . . .

Since Valéry describes Eupalinos as of Megara, and since it was at Megara that the school of Euclid flourished, Valéry's ascription of the name of Eupalinos to the *Encyclopédie Berthelot* dispels the idea of any relation between Eupalinos and Euclid. Finally, to return to the letter to Paul Souday, Valéry said of "these dialogues":

They are works made to order, in which I have not managed or known how to establish a true thought in its most favorable light. I should have tried to show that pure thought and the search for truth in itself can only ever aspire to the discovery or the construction of some *form*.

What, then, are the ideas that Valéry has chosen to be discussed by the shades of Socrates and his friend Phaedrus, as they meet, in our time, in their "dim habitation" on the bank of Ilissus? They are alone and remain alone. Eupalinos does not appear and takes no part in the discussion, unless, as he is spoken of, an image of him passes, like the shade of a shade. The talk is prolonged, and during its course, one or the other speaker propounds ideas. If we attempt to group a number of the ideas propounded, we have something like the following:

There are no details in execution.

Nothing beautiful is separable from life, and life is that which dies.

We must now know what is truly beautiful, what is ugly; what befits man; what can fill him with wonder without confounding him, possess him without stupefying him. . . . It is that which puts him, without effort, above his own nature.

By dint of constructing, . . . I truly believe that I have constructed myself. . . . To construct oneself, to know oneself—are these two distinct acts or not?

What is important for me above all else is to obtain from *that which is going to be,* that it should with all the vigor of its newness satisfy the reasonable requirements of *that which has been.*

O body of mine . . . keep watch over my work. . . . Grant me to find in thy alliance the feeling of what is true; temper, strengthen, and confirm my thoughts.

No geometry without the word.

Nothing can beguile, nothing attract us, . . . nothing by us is chosen from among the multitude of things, and causes a stir in our souls, that was not in some sort pre-existent in our being or secretly awaited by our nature.

An artist is worth a thousand centuries.

Man . . . fabricates by abstraction.

Man can act only because he can ignore.

That which makes and that which is made are indivisible.

The greatest liberty is born of the greatest rigor.

Man's deepest glances are those that go out to the void. They converge beyond the All.

If, then, the universe is the effect of some act; that act itself, the effect of a Being, and of a need, a thought, a knowledge, and a power which belong to that Being, it is then only by an act that you can rejoin the grand design, and undertake the imitation of that which has made all things. And that is to put oneself in the most natural way in the very place of the God.

Now, of all acts the most complete is that of constructing.

But the constructor whom I am now bringing to the fore . . .

takes as the starting point of his act, the very point where the god had left off. . . . Here I am, says the Constructor, I am the act.

Must I be silent, Phaedrus?—So you will never know what temples, what theaters, I should have conceived in the pure Socratic style! . . . And exercising an ever stricter control over my mind, at the highest point I should have realized the operation of transforming a quarry and a forest into an edifice, into splendid equilibriums! . . .

Then out of raw materials I was going to put together my structures entirely ordained for the life and joy of the rosy race of men. . . . But you shall learn no more. You can conceive only the old Socrates, and your stubborn shade. . . .

This is the substance of the dialogue between Socrates and Phaedrus, or, at least, these sayings, taken from their talk, indicate what they have been talking about. And what in fact have they been talking about? And why is Valéry justified when, in his closing words, Socrates says: ". . . all that we have been saying is as much a natural sport of the silence of these nether regions as the fantasy of some rhetorician of the other world who has used us as puppets!" Have we been listening to the talk of men or of puppets? These questions are parts of the fundamental question, What should the shades of men talk about, or in any case what may they be expected, categorically, to talk about, in the Elysian fields? Socrates answers this question in the following manner:

Think you not that we ought now to employ this boundless leisure which death leaves us, in judging and rejudging ourselves unwearyingly, revising, correcting, attempting other answers to the events that took place, seeking, in fine, to defend ourselves by illusions against nonexistence, as the living do against their existence?

This Socratic question (and answer) seems empty. The Elysian fields would be the merest penal habitude, if existence in them was not as absolute as it is supposed to be eternal and if our disillusioned shades were dependent, there, on some fresh illusion to be engendered by them for themselves in that transparent realm. It cannot be said freely that Valéry himself fails to exhibit Socrates and Phaedrus engaged in any such discussion, for as the talk begins to reach its end, there emerges from it an Anti-Socrates, to whom an Anti-Phaedrus is listening, as if their conversation had been, after all, a process of judging and rejudging what they had done in the past, with the object of arriving at a state of mind equivalent to an illusion. The dialogue does not create this impression. It does not seem to us, as we read it, that we are concerned with the fortunes of the selves of Socrates and Phaedrus, notwithstanding that that would be a great concern.

We might well expect an existence after death to consist of the revelation of the truth about life, whether the revelation was instantaneous, complete, and dazzling, or whether it was a continuity of discoveries made at will. Hence when a conversation between Socrates and Phaedrus after death occurs, we somehow expect it to consist of resolutions of our severest philosophical or religious difficulties, or of some of them. The present dialogue, however, is a discussion of aesthetics. It may even be said to be the apotheosis of aesthetics, which is not at all what we have had in mind as that which phantoms talk about. It makes the scene seem more like a place in provincial France than either an archaeological or poetic afterworld. In view of Valéry's reference to "the very admirable Stephanos," it is clear that the scene is the afterworld of today, since Mallarmé died in 1898. The trouble is that our sense of what ought to be discussed in the afterworld is derived from specimens that have fallen into disuse. Analysis of the point would be irrelevant. It seems enough to suppose that to the extent that the dead exist in the mind of the living, they discuss whatever the living discuss, although it cannot be said that they do it in quite the same way, since when Phaedrus told Socrates how Socrates, if he had been an architect, would have surpassed "our most famous builders," Eupalinos included, Socrates replied: "Phaedrus, I beg of you! . . . This subtle matter of which we are now made does not permit of our laughing. I feel I ought to laugh, but I cannot. . . . So refrain!"

This elevation of aesthetics is typical of Valéry's thought. It is itself an act of construction. It is not an imbalance attributable to his nature as a poet. It is a consequence of reasonable conviction on his part. His partiality for architecture was instinctive and declared itself in his youthful *Introduction to the Method of Leonardo da Vinci.* It was not an artificiality contrived to please the company of architects who had commanded *Eupalinos.* It seems most natural that a thinker who had traced so much of man's art to man's body should extend man's art itself to the place of God and in that way should relate man's body to God, in the manner in which this is done in *Eupalinos.* Socrates said: "I cannot think that there exists more than one Sovereign Good."

Phaedrus then spoke of what Eupalinos had said concerning forms and appearances. He repeated the words of Eupalinos:

Listen, Phaedrus . . . that little temple, which I built for Hermes, a few steps from here, if you could know what it means to me! — There where the passer-by sees but an elegant chapel—'t is but a trifle: four columns, a very simple style—there I have enshrined the memory of a bright day in my life. O sweet metamorphosis! This delicate temple, none knows it, is the mathematical image of a girl of Corinth, whom I happily loved. It reproduces faithfully the proportions that were peculiarly hers. It lives for me! It gives me back what I have given it. . . .

Eupalinos had then spoken of buildings that are mute, of others that speak, and of others that sing, for which he gave the reasons.

Socrates interrupted Phaedrus with a reference to his prison, which he called "a drab and indifferent place in itself." But he added, "In truth, dear Phaedrus, I never had a prison other than my body."

Eupalinos had gone on to speak to Phaedrus of the effect on the spirit of the sites of ports: ". . . the presence of the pure horizon, the waxing and the waning of a sail, the emotion that comes of being severed from the earth, the beginning of perils, the sparkling threshold of lands unknown." He did not profess to be able to connect up an analysis with an ecstasy. He said:

I feel my need of beauty, proportionate to my unknown resources, engendering of itself alone forms that give it satisfaction. I desire with my whole being. . . . The powers assemble. The powers of the soul, as you know, come strangely up out of the night. . . . By force of illusion they advance to the very borders of the real. I summon them, I adjure them by my silence. . . .

He continued:

O Phaedrus, when I design a dwelling (whether it be for the gods, or for a man), and when I lovingly seek its form, . . . I confess, how strange soever it may appear to you, *that it seems to me my body is playing its part in the game.*

Eupalinos ended with the prayer to his body, which Socrates called "an unexampled prayer," when Phaedrus repeated it. It is Socrates himself—in the apostrophe to Phaedrus, beginning "O coeternal with me in death," in the closing pages of the dialogue—who says that man by his acts puts himself in the place of God, not meaning that he becomes God but that he puts himself in the very place of God: *la place même du Dieu*.

It follows that for Eupalinos and for men like him what they do is their approach to the divine and that the true understanding of their craft and the total need that they feel to try to arrive at a true understanding of it and also at an exact practice of it are immeasurably the most important things in the world, through which the world itself comes to the place of the divine. The present work has to be read with all this in mind. Any rigorous intellectual discipline in respect to something significant is a discipline in respect to everything significant. Valéry's own discipline appears in every page of the dialogue. The need to understand uncommon things and to manifest that understanding in common things shows itself constantly. The modeling of the cluster of roses is an instance. The comparison of the object found on the shore of the sea, a natural object, with an object made by man is another. The parable of the Phoenician and how he went about making a ship is a third. It is the parable of the artist. The image of the Phoenician's boat recalled to Socrates ". . . the black, loose-flapping sails of the vessel with its load of priests, which as it labored back from Delos, dragging on its oars. . . ."

At this, Phaedrus exclaimed, "How little you seem to relish living your beautiful life over again!"

Socrates then asked, "Is there anything vainer than the shadow of a sage?"

And Phaedrus said, "A sage himself." The image of the

man of action makes the shade of the man of thought regret his life. It is, in a way, the triumphant image of the constructor as it faces the image of the man of thought. Perhaps on his own grounds, it was Valéry, for all his life of study, full of the sea, watching the departure of the Phoenician's supreme boat on its maiden voyage: "Her scarlet cheeks took all the kisses that leapt up to meet her on her course; the well-stretched triangles of her full, hard sails held down her quarter to the wave. . . ."

Is it not possible that one of the most perceptive texts of modern times, although neither immense nor varied, and containing little of life and the nature of man, is yet a masterpiece? Within the limits of the work, Valéry expresses ideas relevant to the thought of his time as it came to consider, with an unprecedented interest, the problems of art. In the dialogue, Socrates speaks of these expatiations as if with a nuance of their triviality. As he continued to probe, his interest heightened to such an extent that he lost his own traditional character; and in this, he became part of the new time in which his shade comes close to us. The nuance of triviality had vanished by the time he reached the noble speech beginning "O coeternal with me in death," when he was ready to say:

The Demiurge was pursuing his own designs, which do not concern his creatures. The converse of this must come to pass. He was not concerned about the troubles that were bound to spring from that very separation which he diverted or perhaps bored himself with making. He has given you the means of living, and even of enjoying many things, but not generally those which you particularly want.

But I come after him. I am he who conceives what you desire a trifle more exactly than you do yourselves. . . . I shall make mistakes sometimes, and we shall have some ruins; but one can always very profitably look upon a work that has failed as a step which brings us nearer to the most beautiful.

In the end, Socrates had become the constructor, and if he had, then Valéry had. The thinker had become the creator. Jean Wahl might have diminished this to a defense mechanism. Perhaps it was an appearance of what Alain called the inimitable visage of the artist. To be a little more exact in quoting Alain, one should say that the creator had asserted its parentage of the thinker, for Alain had spoken of thought as the daughter of poetry in a passage peculiarly applicable to Valéry. He had said that of all the indicators of thought the most sensitive were poets, first because they take risks a little further than logic permits; also because the rule they adopt always carries them a little beyond what they hoped for. Mallarmé and Valéry announce a new climate of thought. They want clear enigmas, those that are developable, that is to say, mathematical. Alain says:

And if it is true, as I believe, that Thought, daughter of Poetry, resembles her mother, we shall see everywhere a clarity of details, a clarity won by conquest, in the place of our vague aspirations; and the young will make us see another manner of believing—which will be a refusal to believe.

Eupalinos is a work of this "clarity of details." This is its precise description. In it Valéry made language itself a constructor, until Socrates asked:

What is there more mysterious than clarity? . . . What more capricious than the way in which light and shade are distributed over hours and over men? . . . Orpheuslike we build, by means of the word, temples of wisdom and science that may suffice for all reasonable creatures. This great art requires of us an admirably exact language.

It has been said that Rilke, who translated so much of Valéry, including *Eupalinos,* felt an intense interest, as a poet, in the language of the work. The page on music—"... a mobile edifice, incessantly renewed and reconstructed within itself, and entirely dedicated to the transformations of a soul"; the page on the sea shore—"This frontier between Neptune and Earth"; the page on in the beginning—"In the beginning ... there was what is: the mountains and the forests ..."—are pages of true poetry. It was natural for such pages to give Rilke pleasure. But what impressed him was what he called the composure and finality of Valéry's language. Rilke read *Eupalinos* when it came out in the *Nouvelle Revue française,* and his translation of it was the last work he did before he died.

It seems sometimes, in the fluidity of the dialogue, as if the discussion was casual and fortuitous or, say, Socratic. But a discussion over which the mind of Socrates presides derives much of its vitality from this characteristic, so that when the talk is over, we have a sense of extended and noble unity, a sense of large and long-considered form.

Chose légère, ailée, sacrée

In 1930, Louis Séchan published a work on *La Danse grecque antique*, which contained a chapter on Valéry's *Dance and the Soul*. M. Séchan was Professor of Greek Language and Literature at the University of Montpellier. He sent a copy of this book to Valéry, who acknowledged it in a letter, which it seems worth while to copy at length, as follows:

I thank you greatly for your attention in sending me your fine work on Greek dancing. I learn from it many things I ignored—and even ignored about myself. Your kind chapter on my little dialogue generously attributes to me much more erudition than I ever possessed. Neither Callimachus nor Lucian, Xenophon nor the Parthenia was known to me; and would not in any case have been of much use to me. Documents in general impede rather than help me. They result in difficulties for me, and consequently in peculiar solutions, in all those compositions in which history must play some part.

In reality, I confined myself to dipping into Emmanuel at the Library, and I left open on my table the book of Marey which I have had for the last thirty years. Those outline drawings of jumping and walking, some memories of ballets were my essential resources. The flutist does come from the Throne. The head compact like a pine cone from a living dancer.

The constant thought of the Dialogue is physiological—from the digestive troubles of the prelude-beginning to the final swoon. Man is slave to the sympathetic and pneumogastric nerves. Sumptuary sensations, the gestures of luxury, and spectacular thoughts exist only by the good favor of these tyrants of our vegetative life. Dance is the type of the runaway.

As for the form of the whole, I have tried to make of the Dialogue itself a sort of ballet of which the Image and the Idea are Coryphaeus in turn. The abstract and the sensible take the lead alternately and unite in the final vertigo.

To sum up: I in no degree strove for historic or technical rigor (and for very good reason). I freely introduced what I needed to maintain my Ballet and vary its figures. This extended to *the ideas themselves*. Here they are *means*. It is true that this idea (that ideas are means) is familiar to me, and perhaps *substantial*. It leads on, moreover, to wicked thoughts about philosophy (cf. "Leonardo and the Philosophers," which I published last year).

I should never have planned to write on the dance, to which I had never given serious thought. Moreover, I considered—and I still do—that Mallarmé had exhausted the subject in so far as it belongs to literature. This conviction made me first refuse the invitation of the *Revue musicale*. Other reasons made me resolve to accept it. What Mallarmé had prodigiously written then became a peculiar condition of my work. I must neither ignore him nor espouse his thought too closely. I adopted the line of introducing, amid the divers interpretations which the three characters give of the dance, the one whose formulation and incomparable demonstration through style are to be found in the *Divagations*.

I have explained myself at considerable length. But I feel I owe this to one who has been such an attentive and even fervent critic of my Dialogue. You have perfectly presented its spirit, which, in truth, is neither *this* nor *that*—neither with Plato, nor according to Nietzsche, but an act of transformation.

The nature of M. Séchan's book can be gathered from Valéry's comment on it. M. Séchan thought that Valéry's attitude toward *Dance and the Soul* as something fortuitous was typical of Valéry. He discussed Mallarmé's remarks in *Divagations* on the dance as corporeal writing or hieroglyphic, and he dwelt on the resemblance between the dance and the meditations of the spirit in moments of tension. He referred to the analysis of *Dance and the Soul* by Paul Souday in the latter's work on Valéry and, in particular, to the contrasting conceptions of the dance by the persons taking part in the present dialogue, thus: the conception of Eryximachus (the Eryximachus of Plato's *Symposium*) that the dance is purely sensory; the conception of Phaedrus (the Phaedrus of *Eupalinos*) that the dance is psychologically evocative; and the conception of Socrates, which reconciles the other two, that the dance is an interpretation of a secret and physical order. And finally M. Séchan speaks of the fact that both Schopenhauer and Nietzsche were influential forces at the time when Valéry was maturing. But he regards *Dance and the Soul* as Apollonian rather than Dionysian, because as Apollonian it corresponds better with the Greek genius. It is, in fact, possible, if only because Valéry published *Eupalinos* and *Dance and the Soul* together and because they seem to be inseparable companions, that Valéry had a sense that *Eupalinos* was Apollonian and that *Dance and the Soul* was Dionysian. On the other hand, it is certain that Valéry's own genius was Apollonian and that the Dionysian did not comport with it, and, with that, the subject may be dismissed.

Dance and the Soul is a lesser work than *Eupalinos,* since it does not contain the proliferation of ideas which characterizes *Eupalinos.* Socrates is always and everywhere proliferation. In this dialogue, however, he confines himself to the proliferation of a single idea. He asks repeatedly the question, "O my friends, what in truth is dance?" and again,

"But what then is dance, and what can steps say?" and again, "O my friends, I am only asking you what is dance. . . ."

While these questions are being asked, a dance is going on, a ballet is being danced. The scene is a banqueting place with a banquet in course. There are servants serving food and no end of wine. The persons are Socrates, Phaedrus, and Eryximachus, great numbers of multicolored groups of smiling figures, whirling and dissolving in enchanted sequences, Athikte, the *première danseuse,* who is commencing, the *musiciennes,* one of whom, coral-rose, is blowing an enormous shell, another, a tall flute-player, who denotes the measure with her toe. Socrates is conscious of ideas that come to him as he watches Athikte and observes the majesty of her movements. Eryximachus exclaims: "Dear Socrates, she teaches us that which we do, showing clearly to our souls that which our bodies accomplish obscurely."

Phaedrus adds: "In which respect this dancer would, according to you, have something Socratic, teaching us, in the matter of walking, to know ourselves a little better."

These remarks illustrate the constant allusions to the dancers which keep the reader of the dialogue in the presence of the dancers. He hears the voices of the speakers and watches the movements of the dancers at one and the same time, without the least confusion, as he would do in reality; and as his interest in what is being said grows greater as the discussion approaches its resolutions, and as his absorption in the spectacle becomes deeper with his increased understanding of it and because of the momentum toward the ultimate climax, he realizes, for the first time, the excitement of a meaning as it is revealed at once in thought and in act.

The work is regenerative. M. Séchan quoted the words of Plato on the poet: *chose légère, ailée, sacrée.* These words apply equally to Valéry's text. Here again we have what we had in *Eupalinos,* the body as source and the act in relation to the body. Socrates says to Eryximachus:

Do you not see then, Eryximachus, that among all intoxications the noblest, the one most inimical to that great tedium, is the intoxication due to acts? Our acts, and more particularly those of our acts which set our bodies in motion, may bring us into a strange and admirable state. . . .

Still speaking to Eryximachus, he made a gesture in the direction of

. . . that ardent Athikte, who divides and gathers herself together again, who rises and falls, so promptly opening out and closing in, and who appears to belong to constellations other than ours—seems to live, completely at ease, in an element comparable to fire—in a most subtle essence of music and movement, wherein she breathes boundless energy, while she participates with all her being in the pure and immediate violence of extreme felicity.

As he continues, he says what sums up his argument and sums up the whole work:

If we compare our grave and weighty condition with the state of that sparkling salamander, does it not seem to you that our ordinary acts, begotten by our successive needs, and our gestures and incidental movements are like coarse materials, like an impure stuff of duration—whilst that exaltation and that vibration of life, that supremacy of tension, that transport into the highest agility one is capable of, have the virtues and the potencies of flame; and that the shames, the worries, the sillinesses, and the monotonous foods of existence are consumed within it, making what is divine in a mortal woman shine before our eyes?

There is a series of speeches by Socrates in the closing pages of the dialogue which are full of the noble rhetoric of the truth. But they are still rhetoric; and it is the presence of this rhetoric of the truth that makes the work regenerative. It is rhetoric to say: "In a sonorous world, resonant and rebounding, this intense festival of the body in the presence of our souls offers light and joy. . . . All is more solemn, all more light, all more lively, all stronger; all is possible in another way; all can begin again indefinitely. . . ." So, too, it is rhetoric to say: "I hear the clash of all the glittering arms of life! . . . The cymbals crush in our ears any utterance of secret thoughts. They resound like kisses from lips of bronze. . . ." It is, however, this rhetoric, the eloquent expression of that which is precisely true, that gives what it expresses an irresistible compulsion as when Socrates says: "A body, by its simple force, and its act, is powerful enough to alter the nature of things more profoundly than ever the mind in its speculations and dreams was able to do!"

While Socrates is pronouncing his subtle and solemn words, our eyes remain fastened on Athikte, while she tries to make us see that which Socrates is seeking to tell us. She moves through jewels, makes gestures like scintillations, filches impossible attitudes from nature, so that Eryximachus says, "Instant engenders form, and form makes the instant visible." She continues to dance until she falls. When she has fallen and lies, white, on the ground, she says something to herself, the simplest possible thing. Phaedrus asks what it is and Eryximachus replies, "She said: 'How well I feel!' "— a remark immense with everything that Socrates himself had been saying a moment or two before. She has spoken in a rhetoric which achieves the pathetic essential almost without speech. It is obvious that this degree of agitation has been reached in what is, after all, an exegetical work, through the form of the work. Valéry's slim and cadenced French adds its own vitality to the original. It seems enough to present the work in this brief manner. André Levinson said in relation to *Dance and the Soul:* "To explain a thing is to deform it; to think is to substitute what is arbitrary for the unknowable truth." What *Dance and the Soul* requires is not so much explanation as—what Valéry called M. Séchan—attentive and fervent critics or, say, readers, willing to experience the transformation which knowing a little about themselves brings about as by miracle or, say, by art.

Man has many ways to attain the divine, and the way of Eupalinos and the way of Athikte and the various ways of Paul Valéry are only a few of them.

SOCRATES AND HIS PHYSICIAN

Socrates

You are leaving me?

Eryximachus

I fly to the bedside of a woman. . . .

Socrates

But, by the Gods, I am still suffering. . . . My head is full and empty; my limbs are broken; my mouth is bitter and dry; and I feel all over a tingling agitation and the most burdensome fatigue, as though I had in myself a baneful principle of all the contradictions. . . .

Eryximachus

You will be better this evening; and well, tomorrow.

Socrates

Stay, I beg you. I am sure you will scarcely be out of reach before my ailments grow worse, I shall have you fetched at top speed. . . . Leave your cloak, your stick, your lantern where they are. . . .

Eryximachus

Another ailment calls me. Someone is writhing on another couch and imploring the Gods to make my steps heard. I adjure you, O Socrates, whom I admire above all mortals, to summon to your aid the sublime calm of your vast intelligence: let it dispel your fears, which I know to be quite vain. Continue to take warm water. Think in moderation. Remain on your bed. Contemplate on the wall the daylight vanishing, and the balance of light and shadow pursuing one another insensibly towards the night. Simple time is a great remedy. I tell you that the fight is ending; you have conquered, and the cause of your body has won. You will be fresh and gay with tomorrow's dawn. So I flee. . . .

Socrates

Go. . . . But do not go until you have given the answer to a question. . . . A single one. You will not leave here until you have satisfied my mind on a point which troubles it. I am anxious to know . . .

Eryximachus

Just see how much better you are. . . . Already our sage revives and recovers in the presence of some thought more universal than the idea of fever and the morose meditation upon fits of nausea.

Socrates

Oh! no. . . . I am not feeling so well! . . . But the ill in me is itself a thinking force. Listen! . . . If you leave me without answering, the question will torment me, fever will return, sleep overwhelm me or flee me, and your ministrations, counteracted by yourself. . . . Listen, Eryximachus.

Eryximachus

Well then. . . . I am listening. But I swear to you that three quarters of my soul is elsewhere.

Socrates

Tell me: you affirm that I am regaining the fullness of good health, and that my being is going to recover all its virtues, as a branch, bent by a child's hand or the weight of a dove, and then restored to itself, returns to its place on the tree, after a few movements of uncertainty. . . .

Eryximachus

I assure you of it.

Socrates

You tell me, moreover, that you are hurrying off to another mortal who calls on your help; and, no doubt, from this one you will go off upon your winged feet to bring solace to a third, and so on and so on. . . . But how can you so acutely foresee in the several cases, and in face of such divers adversities, the destiny of the different ills, the increase or decrease of the intestine difficulties of all these bodies which have only their disorders in common and only anguishes alike?

Eryximachus

Do you not yourself go from idea to idea? Do you not change your interlocutors and therefore your tactics? Do you not know (and know marvelously) that you do not seduce Zeno as you seduce Phaedrus? Do you try to penetrate, to treat, and to cure all souls according to a single method and by the same means?

Socrates

Wait. . . . Do not question me. If your time is precious, fleeting is the time of my thought. If I wish to know something, the very instant of my desire is also the very instant when my mind is about to become most happily imbued with the enlightenment offered it. A mind receives all the better if it finds itself in the state closest to producing, of itself, what it desires. . . . And is this not true of all nourishment, and is it not said of fecundation?

Eryximachus

I have heard it said. . . .

Socrates

Allow me then to express to you in all its freshness what I am curious about. You are my enigma. You are he who does me good or tries to: but I only now want to consider him who possesses the power to do this good, and to do good to many others than myself. It is your art itself which puzzles me. I ask myself how you know what you know, and what kind of a mind can be yours for you to be able to speak to me as you did just now, without falsehood or presumption, when you told me, or foretold me, that I shall be cured tomorrow, and satisfied with my body from the dawn of the day. I marvel at what you must be, you and your medicine, in order to obtain from my nature that blessed oracle and to have a presentiment of its propensity for the better. This body, which is mine, confides and entrusts itself to you and not to myself; to which latter it only addresses itself in the form of troubles, fatigues, and pains, which are as it were the insults and blasphemies which it can utter when it is displeased. It speaks to my mind as to a beast, which one drives without explanations, but by violence and savage abuse; whilst it tells you clearly what it wishes and does not wish, and the why and how of its state. It is strange that you should know a thousand times more than I do about myself, and that I should be as it were transparent to the light of your knowledge, while I am for myself quite obscure and opaque. Nay more: you even see that which I not yet am, and you assign to my body a certain good, to which it must make its way, as though on your orders and at such and such a moment fixed by you. . . . Wait. You look at me as though my astonishment astonished you, and I were putting to you some childish question.

Eryximachus

I am waiting, O greatest among the sages, I am waiting; and true it is that I am astonished. But do not you forget, I beg you, that each of your words uttered *here* adds *there* some grain of unbearable duration to someone's anxious expectation.

Socrates

Listen then. You well know, you who come so often to take your share in the conversations my friends have with me, you know that—once practical things and business are well over—my days are spent in questioning myself, either alone, or through the dialectical detour of well-directed converse, seeking, by every means, to make for myself an idea of myself as right and sincere as possible, since I see no other object worthier to be fathomed. I have not found any other worth living for, for the purpose of a life seems to me to be to use its time and strength to make, or create, or perceive, something which should render quite useless, and even inconceivable and absurd, the rebeginning of an existence. *Living should therefore, in my view, be directed against reliving.* That is to say that a life's course should have as its essential idea a knowledge of oneself so accomplished that nothing can, when it touches its highest point, any more modify its structure, forms, and modes. So it is with the growth of a child, all of whose fumblings and risky experiments converge, from birth, gradually to give it a possession of its body and of sensible things which, when once and for all it has been acquired, can no more increase, nor be modified, nor even be conceived differently.

The experience of this extreme knowledge would also be the last thought possible, and as it were the last drop of the liquid which completely fills a vessel. The measure being quite full, the duration of my life would seem to me to be exactly exhausted.

Now I have done my best, friend Eryximachus, to follow the road to this end. No doubt I could not claim to know my mortal body in detail nor to picture to myself all the chances that can change it. But I flattered myself that my soul would always reduce and master, if not all the powers of my body (since all-powerful sufferings and unbearable ordeals do exist), then at least all that which, deriving from this body, tends to confuse it and lead it into error regarding the True or the Beautiful or the Right. But you are now bringing me to feel great fear about the very substance of my principle and my hope. If you show me you know me better than I do myself, and can foresee even my next mood, seeing me already gay and full of vigor, whilst I find myself at present quite overwhelmed and full of disgust, must I not conclude that my whole effort is puerile, that my intimate tactics vanish in the face of your entirely exterior art, which envelops my body and soul at once in a network of particular points of knowledge woven together, thereby capturing at a single stroke the universe of my person?

Eryximachus

Do not make me so formidable, great Socrates. . . . I am not the monster of knowledge and power which you create for yourself. My limitations are all too certain.

I for my part am concerned only with phenomena, inside the complexity and confusion of which I try to find my bearings, so as to bring as much solace as possible to the humans who consult me; and, in the course of doing so, to cause them the least ill (for the physician must fear his art and not make an unreserved use of its weapons).

It is true I know you better than you do yourself . . . in so far as you are ignorant of yourself; but infinitely less well in so far as you know yourself. I know much better than you what is in your belly and what there is between the bones of your wonderfully gifted head; I can say, with some—though not absolute—assurance, the kind of person you will be, and in what humor, at your next awakening. But what you will do with that humor, and with all the beautiful surprises which it will bring to your mind and which will enchant us in the evenings—all this necessarily escapes me, apart from which your fame would be but mine; and I should even be a More-than-Socrates in the eyes of men and Gods. . . . You are ignorant of yourself, Socrates, in so far as you are a mortal, for your mind in its purity is engaged inside time in separating off its own essence from every condition of perishability: if you knew what I know, you could not know what you know. . . . Adieu. I leave you with your daemon, and your body to the favorable hands of Asclepius.

Socrates

But. . . . He is already far away! . . . I well see that flight is in the nature of physicians. I do not, it is true, know what would happen to medicine and to mortals if to each of them were attached a physician who would not leave him day or night, nor cease to observe him at every instant. This one deserts me. He leaves me divided between what he knows and what I ignore, and on the other hand, what he ignores and what I know. . . . My mind, still rather turbid with clouds which obscure the sense, repeats to itself as an oracle a strange and ambiguous saying: EVERYTHING RESTS ON ME—I HANG UPON A THREAD. . . .

PRIDE FOR PRIDE

Anaxagoras

If you are right, since you are not me you cannot be truly right, O Socrates. I therefore must further reflect. Taking up the thread of what you have said to me, and setting out from the state into which you have put my thought, after having first opposed and overcome it, I needs must discover a final reason in myself which at one and the same time contains your own and yet justifies my previous opinion. And that at the risk of my death. For how would my existence otherwise make sense?

Socrates

What pride! Anaxagoras. . . . Pride is the feeling of being born for something which we alone can conceive, and this a thing greater and more important than any other. Nothing ought to be greater than the thing I would do . . . (and cannot).

The thing which I wish must always be superior to that which anyone else wishes. Such is pride. It does not emanate from things already done nor from that which one is. But my ideal is infinitely above yours, since it is mine—solely because it is mine. . . .

COLLOQUY WITHIN A BEING

"The dawn unveiled to me the whole of hostile day."

A

Come. . . . Emerge from the instant. . . . Compose your powers. . . . Disengage who you are from the living mud which lies, in the form of a man cast down and abandoned, in the disorder of the bed linen. . . . Be reborn! It is time. Night is decomposing. It is rapidly losing its stars, and the poison of the coming day penetrates it. The light steals into the deep substance of the gloom, corrupting its solemn unity. As products of this corruption one sees appearing, here and there, rough drafts of things, first symptoms of the objects and beings which are going to require responses and acts from you. . . .

B

Have pity! I cannot. You are asking nothing less than the impossible! The weight of my body is that of the whole earth beneath me. How do you expect me to raise myself, lift at once all the being and all the nonbeing which are intimately confounded in me? The least effort, the least essay of the spirit exceed the means of this moment. Leave me. . . . Oh! Leave me!

A

No. I shall urge you to reconstruct yourself.

17

B

But I tell you I am IMPOSSIBILITY. . . . Do you conceive
that a stone can modify itself in itself by itself to the extent of
finding in itself the means for breaking with the ground and
springing prodigiously aloft? . . . Listen! Leave me. I am as
though absent in my presence, and scarce half-present in my
absence. There are no bonds in me between *that which sees,
wishes, lasts, changes, knows* and *that which would do*. . . . I do
not distinguish who I was, who I am, who I can be. . . .
Tormentor that you are, you oblige me to answer you, and
I find it so painful that I feel tears of impotence and refusal
come to my eyes. . . .

A

Weep, but live! . . . Emerge from your larvalike state.
Unravel me that miserable mixture of equivalent sensations,
of memories without employment, dreams without credit,
conjectures without consistency. . . . Summon and rally all
those little unfocused forces which are adrift in your fatigue.
Your weakness is simply their confusion. Come, divide me
up all these species: collect your energies that are of the same
kind; no longer mix up the true with the false; each must
serve in its turn! Organize the several parts of complex time
which allow you to bring *that which is not* to act upon *that
which is*, and *that which is* upon *that which is not*. . . . Order
well your legs and your arms, and feel your power to the
very extremities of your empire over those limbs. Take
possession of your look and *make space*, instead of under-
going all the accidents of colored extension. . . . Draw then,
with this regard as it moves, the precise outline of objects.
Make sure, too, of your inner powers. Exact, exercise, excite
the general freedom of the terms and forms of your lan-

guage; awaken its resources for the combination, transposition, articulation of ideas and for the distinguishing of concepts. . . .

B

Be still. . . .

A

That is not all. . . .

B

What more do you want of me? Are you yourself distinguishing as to whether you are resuscitating or murdering me?

A

That is not all, I tell you. Stir up your thought. Apply to some point which begins to dawn in your mind the prick of desire and the power of duration through which the totality of similitudes, the space for resonance, the quantity of possibilities infused in what you are will dispose themselves so as to favor the complete development of this germ. . . .

B

Be still! . . . The mere recalling of my forces weighs me down. You constrain me to measure the immense trouble one must take in order to cease being half dead. . . . Leave me, at least, all the time I need to return without too much stress or regret from the condition of a thing to that of a beast, and from beast to man, and from man to SELF, to the unique. . . .

A

I see that the hardest part is over. You are leaning on your elbow.

B

Alas, yes. . . . I am waking up. . . . I am no longer balanced as it were between all and zero: a mere trifle would have rejected me into the nothingness of my sleep; a mere trifle would have made me arise, built of strength, ready to live. . . .

A

You are going to differ from yourself as differs from a slack rope that *selfsame* rope when taut.

B

Perhaps. But I feel myself at first strangely a prey to my powers. My memory obsesses me. My intellect makes demands, and my virtue of action abounds in my muscles which it hardens; without an aim as yet. . . . *To feel, to be able, to will, to know, to have a duty to.* . . . All these demons of day stretch their limbs.

A

Consider this virgin day. . . .

B

Virgin as the street. . . . Scarcely do I think of it than I distinguish, in the first layers of my mind, divers cares formed, beings which *are awaiting me;* and above all some very troublesome thing, very difficult to do just today.

A

What thing?

B

I tell you I do not know yet. It is still veiled. A certainty without features. It will shortly take on all its equipment of time, place, cause, and executory force. . . . To think that I have kept *that* within me all night; that I awaken, and that *that* awakens; and that a day which does not yet exist is already quite poisoned by it! . . .

A

Await the event. Perhaps, towards evening, you will be pleased about this affair once it is finished, and, perhaps, pleased about yourself.

B

Oh. . . . Why become again? Why have you drawn me from this phosphorescent mire between waking and sleep? To become SO AND SO. . . . He who has my name, who is stamped with my habits, my difficulties, my opinions, loaded with so many things which could have been quite otherwise, which I feel to be quite accidental, and yet which define ME. Why? Why give me back to the known sun, and to the same self known only too well? If one falls asleep, is that not a kind of demonstration of the perfect sufficiency of having lived the day one has just lived? Does not an experience of some hours say everything? *Intelligenti pauca.* . . . How often I feel I know myself by heart!

A

Nothing could be better—as they say in Molière. . . . I see that you are reasoning, that you are composing ideas and giving form to your thought. *Utilizable energy* is soon going to superabound in your economy, and by means of projects, decisions, creations, and destructions—you yourself will provide the answer to the question which you are putting me (or putting to yourself), and which suffers no other reply. *There is no "why" when life is involved.*

B

You are perhaps right.

A

You seem to me quite awake, reconstituted, reconstructed. . . .

B

By what sign do you recognize it?

A

By our being in agreement. So there is no place between us for VAGUE THINGS; for questions which are answers, for answers which are questions; for the problems which are in search of their data; for the terms which those who employ them think richer than themselves; for the simplicity which believes in *knowing without being able*. . . . What are you doing? You are jumping out of bed?

B

Up. . . . I am up. I strike with my bare heel the reality of the sensible world. . . .

A

It is a kind of *coup d'état*. . . . And then? . . . You dress?

B

Not quite yet. The sea is close at hand. "I rush to the waves to re-emerge alive."

A

And then?

B

And then. . . . I shall do what must be done. I suddenly feel in myself an extraordinary energy. I find myself loaded with life and almost embarrassed with an invading freedom to think and act, which is strongly provoked by the imminence of the difficulties and the troubles which just now weighed down my soul.

A

Be careful! I am delighted to see you so different from him whom I was tearing away with such difficulty from the state of confused life. Truly I rejoice in your metamorphosis. You were nothing, and now you would do everything! But beware. . . . Do not abuse this vigor. Evening exists. It comes always.

B

Do you think my lucidity does not see it come? Do you think it does not think its own twilight—and even admire it? Is it not a major kind of marvel to think one possesses in oneself the means for disappearing from oneself—whilst all things, of whatever kind they be, caught as it were in a one and only net which draws them insensibly towards the shade—the persons, thoughts, desires, values, the goods, and the ills, and my body and the gods, retire, dissolve, grow dim, and are annihilated together? . . . Nothing has taken place. Everything is wiped away at once. Beautiful? When the ship sinks, the sky vanishes and the sea goes up in mist. . . .

But just now, friend, look how hard this fist is. It strikes the table. The same force is in my heart, which is big as my fist, and beats the full rhythm of my might! I am measure

and excess of measure, rigor and tenderness, desire and disdain; I waste and I accumulate; I love and hate myself,
and I feel myself, from top to toe, accepting myself as I am,
whatever I may be, responding with my whole being to the
simplest question in the world: *what can a man do?*

DANCE AND THE SOUL

Eryximachus

O Socrates, I die! . . . Give me Spirit! Pour me out Ideas! . . . Bring to my nostrils your pungent enigmas! . . . This pitiless repast outdoes all conceivable appetite and all believable thirst! . . . What a fate—to succeed to good things and be the heir of a digestion! . . . My soul is nothing now but the dream dreamt by matter struggling with itself! . . . O good things, O too good things, I bid you pass! . . . Alas! since as day declined we have fallen a prey to what is best in the world, this terrible best, multiplied by duration, imposes its unbearable presence. . . . And now I perish from a mad longing for things that are dry, and serious, and utterly spiritual! . . . Let me come and sit beside you and Phaedrus; and grant that—my back deliberately turned upon those perpetually recurring viands and those inexhaustible urns—I hold out the supreme cup of my spirit to catch your words. What were you saying?

Phaedrus

Nothing as yet. We were watching our fellows eat and drink. . . .

Eryximachus

But Socrates cannot but have been meditating upon something? . . . Can he ever remain solitary with himself—and silent to his very soul! He was tenderly smiling at his daemon upon the dark borderland of this feast. What are your lips murmuring, dear Socrates?

Socrates

They say to me—gently: the man who eats is the most just of men. . . .

Eryximachus

There we have the enigma already, and the appetite of the spirit which it is destined to whet. . . .

Socrates

The man who eats, say my lips, feeds his own goods and ills. Each morsel which he feels melt away and dissipate within him brings new strength to his virtues, but also—indifferently—to his vices. It provides sustenance for his torments just as it fattens his hopes; and is divided somewhere between passions and reasons. Love needs it, as does hate; and my joy and my bitterness, my memory together with my projects, share between them like brothers the very substance of one and the same mouthful. What think you, son of Acumenos?

Eryximachus

I think that I think as you do.

Socrates

O physician that you are, I was silently admiring the acts of all these feeding bodies. Each of them, all unknowing, fairly gives its due to each chance of life, to each germ of death within itself. They know not what they are doing, but they do it like gods.

Eryximachus

I have long observed it: all that enters into man very soon comports itself as the Fates decree. It is as though the isthmus of the gullet were the threshold of capricious necessities and organized mystery. There the will ceases, and the sure empire of knowledge. That is why, in the practice of my art, I have given up all those inconstant drugs which the general run of practitioners agree to impose upon the diversity of their patients; and I keep strictly to obvious remedies. Compounded in equal parts, one for one, as their nature allows.

Phaedrus

What remedies?

Eryximachus

There are eight: hot, cold; abstinence and its contrary; air and water; rest and movement. That is all.

Socrates

But for the soul there are only two, Eryximachus.

Phaedrus

What are they?

Socrates

Truth and falsehood.

Phaedrus

How is that?

Socrates

Are they not to one another as waking is to sleeping? Do you not seek awakening and the sharpness of light when harrowed by a bad dream? Are we not resuscitated by the sun in person, and fortified by the presence of solid bodies?— Do we not, on the other hand, ask of sleep and dreams to dispel our troubles and to suspend the sufferings which pursue us in the world of daylight? And so we flee from the one into the other, invoking day in the middle of the night; imploring darkness, on the contrary, while we have light; anxious to know, yet only too happy to ignore, we seek in what is, a remedy for what is not; and in what is not, a relief for what is. Now the real, now illusion is our refuge; and the soul has finally no other resource but the true, which is her weapon—and falsehood, which is her armor.

Eryximachus

Agreed. . . . But do you not fear, dear Socrates, a certain consequence upon that thought of yours?

Socrates

What consequence?

Eryximachus

This: that truth and falsehood tend to the same end. . . . It is one and the same thing which, according to the way it sets about it, makes us liars or truthful; and just as at times the hot and at times the cold now attack and now defend us, so the true and the false, and the opposing wills that pertain to them.

Socrates

Nothing is more certain. I cannot help it. Life itself wills it so: you, Eryximachus, know better than I that it makes use of everything. Everything helps it never to conclude. Which means that its only conclusion is itself. . . . For is not life that mysterious movement which, taking the detour of everything that happens, transforms me unceasingly into myself and brings me back, promptly enough, to the same Socrates, so that I may find him again—so that, imagining perforce that I recognize him, I may *be*?—Life is a woman who dances and who would cease divinely to be a woman if she could obey her bound up to the skies. But as we can go on to infinity neither in dream nor in waking, so she likewise always becomes herself again; ceases to be snowflake, bird, idea; ceases, in fine, to be all that it pleases the flute that she should be; for the same Earth which sent her forth calls her back and returns her, all breathless, to her woman's nature and to her friend. . . .

Phaedrus

A miracle! . . . Marvelous man! . . . Almost a true miracle! Scarce do you open your lips, and you call into being what is needed! . . . Your images cannot remain images! . . . And lo! just as though from thy creative lips was born the bee, and bee upon bee—behold the winged choir of the famed dancers! . . . The air hums and resounds with intimations of the spectacle about to be! . . . All the torches awaken. . . . The mutterings of the sleepers are transformed; and upon the walls atremble with flames stir the vast shadows of drunkards in uneasy amaze! . . . See that troop, half-light, half-solemn!—coming in like souls!

Socrates

By the gods, the bright dancers! . . . How lively and gracious an introduction of the most perfect thoughts! . . . Their hands speak, and their feet seem to write. What precision in these beings who school themselves to make such felicitous use of their tender strength! . . . All my difficulties abandon me, and at this moment not one problem troubles me, so happily do I obey the mobility of those figures! Here certainty is a sport; it is as though knowledge has found its act, and intelligence on a sudden gives its consent to spontaneous graces. . . . See this one! . . . the slenderest and the one most absorbed in pure rightness. . . . Who is she? . . . She is deliciously hard and inexpressibly supple. . . . She yields, she borrows, and gives back the cadence so exactly that if I shut my eyes, I see her exactly with my hearing. I follow her, I find her again, I can never lose her; and if I stop my ears and look at her, so wholly is she rhythm and music that it is impossible for me not to hear the cithers.

Phaedrus

It is Rhodopis, I think, who enchants you.

Socrates

Rhodopis' ear and ankle, then, are wonderfully wed. . . . How exact she is! . . . Old time grows young again!

Eryximachus

But no, Phaedrus! . . . Rhodopis is the other, so soft, so easy for the eye to caress indefinitely.

Socrates

Who then is the slim monster of suppleness?

Eryximachus

Rhodonia.

Socrates

Rhodonia's ear and ankle, then, are wonderfully wed.

Eryximachus

I know them all, for the matter of that, and each by herself. I can tell you their names. They go very well into a little poem which is easily remembered: Nips, Nephoë, Nema—Nikteris, Nephele, Nexis—Rhodopis, Rhodonia, Ptile. . . . As for the little boy dancer who is so ugly, they call him Nettarion. . . . But the Queen of the Choir has not yet entered.

Phaedrus

And who is it who reigns over these bees?

Eryximachus

The astonishing and extreme dancer, Athikte!

Phaedrus

How you know them!

Eryximachus

All this charming company have plenty of other names! Some come from their parents, and others from their intimates. . . .

Phaedrus

That is what you are. . . . You know them much too well!

Eryximachus

I know them much better than well, and in some sense a little better than they know themselves. O Phaedrus, am I not *the physician?*—In me, through me, all the secrets of medicine are secretly bartered for all the secrets of the dancer! They call me for everything. Sprains, spots, phantasms, heartaches, the varied accidents of their profession (including substantial ones which derive easily from a most mobile career)—and their mysterious ailments; even jealousy, be it artistic or sentimental; even dreams! . . . Do you know they have only to whisper to me some dream which torments them for me to conclude, for example, that some tooth is affected?

Socrates

Admirable man, who know teeth by dreams, think you that all those of philosophers are decayed?

Eryximachus

May the gods preserve me from the bite of Socrates!

Phaedrus

But look at those arms and legs! . . . A few women are doing a thousand things. A thousand torches, a thousand ephemeral peristyles, trellises, and columns. . . . The images melt away and vanish. . . . And now we have a grove of beautiful branches, all stirred by the breezes of music! Is there any dream, O Eryximachus, that signifies more torments, or more a dangerous affection of the mind?

Socrates

But this is precisely the contrary of a dream, dear Phaedrus.

Phaedrus

But *I* dream. . . . I dream of the softness, multiplying itself indefinitely, of these encounters, and of these interchanges of virgin forms. I dream of those inexpressible contacts which take place in the soul between the beats, between the whitenesses and passes of those limbs moving in measure, and the strains of that muffled symphony on which all things seem to be painted and transported. . . . I breathe in, like

34

some heady and composite aroma, the mingling fragrance of this female enchantment; and my presence strays bewildered in this labyrinth of graces, wherein each dancer is lost with her companion and appears again with another.

Socrates

O soul vowed to voluptuousness, see then here the contrary of a dream and the absence of chance. . . . But what, Phaedrus, is the contrary of a dream if not some other dream? . . . A dream of vigilance and tension dreamt by Reason herself!—And what would such a Reason dream?— If a Reason were to dream—a Reason hard, erect, eyes armed, mouth closed, as though mistress of her lips—would not the dream she dreamt be what we now see—this world of exact forces and studied illusions?—A dream, a dream, but a dream interpenetrated with symmetries, all order, acts, and sequences! . . . Who knows what august Laws here dream that they have put on clear countenances, and that they are of one accord in the design of manifesting to mortals in what way the real, the unreal, and the intelligible can fuse and combine as the power of the Muses dictates?

Eryximachus

It is most true, O Socrates, that the treasure of these images is beyond price. . . . Think you not that the thought of the Immortals is precisely that which we see, and that that infinity of these noble similitudes, the conversions, the inversions, the inexhaustible diversions which answer one another and are deduced from each other before our eyes, transport us into the realm of divine knowledge?

Phaedrus

How pure it is, how graceful, the little temple they now form—a rosy round—turning slowly as the night! . . . It resolves into girls, tunics fly, and the gods seem to be changing their mind! . . .

Eryximachus

The divine thought is at present that abundance of multi-colored groups of smiling figures; again and again it engenders those delightful patterns of movement, swirl upon voluptuous swirl formed of two or three bodies and indissoluble henceforth. . . . One of the dancers is as imprisoned. Nevermore will she escape their enchanted chains! . . .

Socrates

But what are they doing all of a sudden? . . . They mingle confusedly, they flee! . . .

Phaedrus

They fly to the doors. They bow in welcome.

Eryximachus

Athikte! Athikte! . . . O gods! . . . The quivering Athikte!

Socrates

She is nothing.

Phaedrus

Little bird!

Socrates

A thing without a body!

Eryximachus

A thing without a price!

Phaedrus

O Socrates, it is as though she were obeying invisible figures!

Socrates

Or yielding to some noble destiny!

Eryximachus

Look! Look! . . . She begins, do you see? with a walk all divine: a simple circular walk. . . . She begins with her art at its highest; she walks naturally on the summit she has attained. This second nature is what is farthest removed from the first, but they must be so like as to be mistaken the one for the other.

Socrates

I enjoy as none other that magnificent freedom. The others now are held motionless and as though enchanted. The flute-girls listen to their own playing, but do not lose her from sight. . . . They are tied to their task, and seem to insist upon the perfection of their accompaniment.

Phaedrus

One, of pink coral, curiously bowed, blows an enormous shell.

Eryximachus

The very tall flutist with slender thighs, close-twined together, stretches out her elegant foot, tapping the beat with her toe. . . . O Socrates, what say you of the dancer?

Socrates

Eryximachus, this little being stirs one to thought. . . . It gathers to itself, it assumes a majesty which was confusedly present in all of us and imperceptibly inhabited the actors of this orgy. . . . A simple walk, and lo, she is a goddess; and we almost gods! . . . A simple walk, the simplest chain of steps! . . . It is as though she purchased space with equal and exquisite acts, and coined with her heel, as she walked, the ringing effigies of movement. She seems to reckon and count out in pieces of pure gold what we thoughtlessly spend in vulgar change of steps, when we walk to any end.

Eryximachus

Dear Socrates, she teaches us that which we do, showing clearly to our souls that which our bodies accomplish obscurely. In the light of her legs, our immediate movements appear to us as miracles. They astound us, in fine, as much as they ought to do.

Phaedrus

In which respect this dancer would, according to you, have something Socratic—teaching us, in the matter of walking, to know ourselves a little better.

Eryximachus

Just so. Our steps are so easy and familiar to us that they never have the honor to be considered in themselves, and as strange acts (unless, being infirm or crippled, we are led by deprivation to admire them). . . . Us in the simplicity of our ignorance they lead as they know how; and according to the ground, the goal, the humor, the state of the man, or even the lighting of the way, they are what they are: we lose them without a thought.

But consider the perfect progress of Athikte, over the faultless floor, which is free, fair, and hardly elastic. Upon that mirror of her forces she places with symmetry her alternating tread; the heel pouring the body towards the toe, the other foot passing and receiving the body, and pouring it onwards again; and so on and on; whilst the adorable crest of her head traces in the eternal present the brow, as it were, of an undulating wave.

As the surface is here in some sort absolute, being scrupulously disengaged from all causes of rhythmlessness and incertitude, this monumental march which has but itself for end and whence all variable impurities have disappeared becomes an universal model.

See what beauty, what full security of soul comes of the length of her noble strides. The amplitude of her steps accords with their number, which emanates directly from the music. But number and length are, again, in secret harmony with height. . . .

Socrates

You speak so well of these things, learned Eryximachus, that I cannot but see them in agreement with your thought. I contemplate this woman who is walking and yet gives me the sense of the motionless. It is this equality of measure alone that holds me. . . .

Phaedrus

She pauses, in the midst of these commensurable graces. . . .

Eryximachus

And now you will see!

Phaedrus

She shuts her eyes. . . .

Socrates

She is entirely in her closed eyes, and quite alone with her soul, in the bosom of the most intimate attention. . . . She feels in herself that she is becoming some event.

Eryximachus

But wait for. . . . Silence, silence!

Phaedrus

Delicious instant. . . . This silence is contradiction. . . . How can one avoid shouting: Silence!

Socrates

Instant entirely virginal. Instant when something must break in the soul, in our expectation, in this assembly. . . . Something break. . . . And yet, it is also like a welding.

Eryximachus

O Athikte! How you excel in imminence!

Phaedrus

Music gently seems to seize her again in another way, lifts her up. . . .

Eryximachus

Music changes her soul.

Socrates

In this moment that is about to die, ye are, O Muses, mistresses all-powerful!

Delicious suspense of breath and of the heart! . . . Gravity

falls at her feet—as is marked by that great veil which drops
noiselessly. Her body must be seen only in movement.

Eryximachus

Her eyes have returned to the light. . . .

Phaedrus

Let us enjoy to the full this most delicate instant when
she changes her purpose! . . . Just as the bird, having reached
the very edge of the roof, breaks with the splendid marble,
and falls into flight. . . .

Eryximachus

I like nothing so much as what is about to happen; and
even in love, I find nothing that surpasses in delight the very
first feelings. Of all the hours of the day, dawn is my favorite. That is why I wish to see with a tender emotion
sacred movement dawn upon this living being. See! . . . It is
born of that sliding glance which invincibly draws onward
the head with its soft nostrils towards the shoulder shining in
the light. . . . And the whole lovely fiber of her smooth, muscular body, from the nape of her neck to the heel of her
foot, progressively expresses and twists itself; all is aquiver.
. . . Slowly she traces a bound about to be born. . . . She
forbids us to breathe until the instant she springs, responding
by a sudden act to the awaited yet unawaited clash of the
rending cymbals! . . .

Socrates

Oh! There at last she is, entering on the exception and
penetrating the impossible! How much alike are our souls,
O my friends, in the presence of this wonder, which is

41

equal and entire, for each of them! . . . How they drink in together what is beautiful!

Eryximachus

Her whole being becomes dance, and wholly vows itself to total movement!

Phaedrus

First she seems, with her steps charged with spirit, to efface from the earth all folly, all fatigue. . . . And see, she is fashioning a dwelling for herself, a little above things— as though making herself a nest within her white arms. . . . But at this moment would you not say that she is spinning with her feet an indefinable carpet of sensations? . . . She crosses, she uncrosses, she weaves the warp of the earth with the woof of duration. . . . O charming workmanship, most precious task of her intelligent toes which attack, which elude, which knot and unknot, which chase each other and take to flight! . . . How skillful they are, how lively, pure artificers of the delights of time lost! . . . The two feet babble together, and bicker like doves! . . . The same point of ground makes them contend, as for a grain of corn! . . . They take off together and clash in mid-air yet again! . . . By the Muses, never have feet made my lips more envious!

Socrates

Here then we have your lips envying the eloquence of these miraculous feet! Fain would you feel their wings in your words, and adorn what you say with figures lively as their leaps!

Phaedrus

I? . . .

Eryximachus

He was thinking only of covering with kisses those turtledoves of feet! . . . An effect of the passionate attention he gives to the spectacle of the dance. What more natural, Socrates, what more ingenuously mysterious? . . . Our Phaedrus is quite dazzled with those points and glittering pirouettes, which are the rightful pride of the tips of the toes of Athikte; he devours them with his eyes, his face strains towards them—and he thinks to feel upon his lips the agile onyx run! —Do not try to excuse yourself, dear Phaedrus, nor feel the very least confusion! . . . You have experienced nothing that was not both lawful and obscure, and thus conforming perfectly to the human machine. Are we not organized fantasy? And is not our living system functioning incoherency, disorder in action? Do not events, desires, ideas interchange within us in the most necessary and incomprehensible ways? . . . What cacophony of causes and effects! . . .

Phaedrus

But you have yourself very well explained what I innocently felt. . . .

Socrates

Dear Phaedrus, in truth, you were not moved without some reason. The more I look at this ineffable dancer, the more I too converse of marvels with myself. I am troubled to conceive how nature has contrived to enclose in a girl, so frail, so refined, this monster of force and of promptitude? Hercules changed to a swallow—is there such a myth? —And can this little head, compact like a young pine cone, infallibly beget the myriads of questions and answers that link her limbs, and those dizzy gropings it produces and reproduces, repudiating them incessantly, receiving them from music and giving them back at once to the light?

Eryximachus

I for my part think of the power of the insect, whose wings' myriad vibrations sustain its fanfare, weight, and courage! . . .

Socrates

She struggles in the meshes of our gaze, like a captured fly. But my curious mind pursues her on the web, and would devour what she accomplishes!

Phaedrus

Dear Socrates, can you never enjoy anything but yourself?

Socrates

O my friends, what in truth is dance?

Eryximachus

Is it not what we see? —What clearer expression of dancing do you want than dancing itself?

Phaedrus

Our Socrates cannot rest until he has seized the soul of all things: if not, indeed, the soul of the soul!

Socrates

But what then is dance, and what can steps say?

Phaedrus

Oh! let us enjoy yet a little, with simplicity, these fair acts! . . . To right, to left; forward, backward; upwards and

44

downwards, she seems to be offering gifts, perfumes, incense, kisses, and her life itself, to all the points of the sphere, and to the poles of the universe. . . .

She traces roses, interlacings, stars of movement, magic precincts. . . . She leaps from circles she has scarcely closed. . . . She leaps and runs after phantoms! . . . She plucks a flower, which forthwith is simply a smile! . . . Oh! how she protests her nonexistence by an inexhaustible lightness! . . . She is adrift in the midst of sounds, she saves herself by a thread. . . . The succorable flute has rescued her! O melody! . . .

Socrates

Now it is as though all around her were nothing but specters. . . . She creates them as she flees them; but if, of a sudden, she turns about, she seems to us to be in the presence of the immortals! . . .

Phaedrus

Is she not the soul of fable, and the runaway through all the gates of life?

Eryximachus

Do you think she knows anything of it? and that she imagines she is engendering other prodigies than beats, and double beats, the highest of kicks,—all laboriously learnt during her apprenticeship?

Socrates

It is true one can undoubtedly also consider things in this light. . . . A cold eye would without difficulty see her as demented, this woman strangely uprooted, who wrests herself incessantly away from her own form, whilst her limbs— gone mad—seem to dispute earth and air; and her head, thrown back, trails on the ground her loosened hair; and one of her legs takes the place of that head; and her finger traces I know not what signs in the dust! . . . After all, why all this? —It is enough for the soul to remain motionless and to withhold itself, for it to conceive only the strangeness and disgust of this ridiculous agitation. . . . Should you but will it, O my soul, all this is absurd!

Eryximachus

You can, then, according to your mood, understand, not understand; find something beautiful or ridiculous, as you please?

Socrates

It must of necessity be so. . . .

Phaedrus

Do you mean, dear Socrates, that your reason considers dance a stranger, whose language it scorns, whose behavior seems to it inexplicable, if not shocking; if not, indeed, altogether obscene?

Eryximachus

Reason, sometimes, seems to me to be the faculty our soul possesses of understanding nothing about our body! . . .

Phaedrus

But me, Socrates, the contemplation of the dancer makes conceive many things, and many relationships between things, which on the spot become my own thought and think in some sort in Phaedrus' stead. I find lights which I should never have gained from the presence of my soul alone. . . .

Just now, for instance, Athikte seemed to me to represent

love. —What love? —Not this one, or that; not some miserable intrigue! —For sure, she was not playing the role of a lover. . . . No mime, no theater! No, no! no fictions!' Why feign, my friends, when at our disposal there are measure and movement, which are what is real in the real? . . . She was love in its very being, then! —But what is love? —Of what is it made? —How define, how paint it? —Well do we know that the soul of love is the invincible difference of lovers, while its subtle matter is the identity of their desires. Dance must therefore, by the subtlety of its lines, by the divineness of its upsurgings, by the delicacy of its tiptoe pauses, bring forth that universal creature which has neither body nor features, but which has gifts, days, and destinies—that has life and death; and which is even only life and death, for desire once born knows neither sleep nor respite.

That is why the dancer alone can make love visible by her beautiful acts. Her whole self, O Socrates, was love! . . . She was toyings and tears, and unavailing feints! Charms, falls, offerings; and surprises, and yes's and no's, and steps sadly lost. . . . She was celebrating all the mysteries of absence and presence; she seemed sometimes to be hovering on the brink of ineffable catastrophes! . . . But now, as a thank offering to Aphrodite, look at her. Is she not of a sudden a very wave of the sea? —Now heavier than her body, now lighter—she bounds, as though dashed from a rock; she softly subsides. . . . She is a wave!

Eryximachus

Phaedrus will, at all costs, have her represent something!

Phaedrus

What do you think, Socrates?

Socrates

Whether she represents anything?

Phaedrus

Yes. Do you think she represents something?

Socrates

Nothing, dear Phaedrus. But everything, Eryximachus. As well love as the sea, and as life itself, and thoughts. . . . Do you not feel she is the pure act of metamorphosis?

Phaedrus

Divine Socrates, you know what simple and singular confidence I have placed, since I have known you, in your incomparable lights: I cannot hear you without believing you, nor believe you without delighting in myself as believing you. But that the dancing of Athikte represents nothing, and is not, above all things, an image of the transports and graces of love is something I find almost unbearable to hear. . . .

Socrates

I have not yet said anything so cruel! —O my friends, I am only asking you what is dance; each of you respectively appears to know; but to know it quite separately! The one tells me that it is what it is, and can be reduced to what our eyes see here; and the other holds very firmly that it represents something, and is therefore not entirely in itself, but principally in us. As for me, my friends, my uncertainty is intact! . . . My thoughts are many in number—which is never a good sign! . . . Many, confused, pressing around me with equal insistence. . . .

Eryximachus

You complain of being rich!

Socrates

Opulence renders immobile. But my desire is movement, Eryximachus. . . . I should now have need of that delicate power which is peculiar to the bee, as it is the sovereign good of the dancer. . . . My mind would need that force and concentrated movement which suspends the insect above the multitude of flowers; which make of it the vibrant arbiter of the diversity of their corollas; which present it as it wills to this or that flower, to that rose a little farther off; and which allow it to touch it fleetingly, to flee it, or to penetrate it. . . . These forces suddenly remove him from the one he has finished loving, just as they bring it back to that flower forthwith, if he repents having left in it some honey whose memory follows him and whose sweetness haunts him during the rest of his flight. . . . Or I should need, O Phaedrus, the subtle displacement of the dancer who, gliding in among my thoughts, awakes each of them delicately in turn, making them rise from under the shadow of my soul, and appear in the light of your minds, in the happiest of all possible orders.

Phaedrus

Speak, speak. . . . I see the bee on your lips, and the dancer in your gaze.

Eryximachus

Speak, O Master of the divine art of trusting the idea as it comes to birth! . . . Ever fortunate author of the marvelous consequences of a dialectical accident! . . . Speak! Draw the golden thread. . . . Bring to us from out of the depths of your absences some living truth!

Phaedrus

Chance is on your side. . . . It changes insensibly into wisdom, as you pursue it with your voice into the labyrinth of your soul!

Socrates

Well, before anything else, I mean to consult our physician!

Eryximachus

It is as you will, dear Socrates.

Socrates

Tell me then, son of Acumenos, O Therapeut Eryximachus, you for whom most bitter drugs and obscure aromatics have so few hidden virtues that you use them not; you, then, who possessing as fully as any man alive all the secrets of art and of nature, yet never prescribe, nor commend, balms or boluses, or mysterious masticks; you who, furthermore, put no trust in elixirs, nor believe in secretly administered philters; O you who heal without electuaries, who disdain everything which—be it powders, drops, gum, curds, flakes or gems or crystals—clings to the tongue, pierces the olfactory cavities, touches the springs of sneezing or nausea, kills or quickens; tell me, then, dear friend Eryximachus, of all healers the most learned in curative substances, tell me this: know you not, from among so many that are active and efficient, from among those masterly preparations which your science contemplates as vain or detestable weapons in the arsenal of the pharmacopoeia—tell me then, do you not know some specific remedy, or some exact antidote, for that evil amongst all evils, that poison of poisons, that venom inimical to all nature? . . .

Phaedrus

What venom?

Socrates

. . . Which is called: *the weariness of living*? —I mean, understand me, not the passing weariness, the tedium which comes of fatigue, or that of which we see the germ or know the limits; but that perfect tedium, that pure tedium which does not come from misfortune or infirmity, and which is compatible with the happiest of all conditions that we may contemplate—that tedium, in fine, whose substance is none other than life itself, and which has no other second cause than the clear-sightedness of the man who is alive. This absolute tedium is in itself nothing other than life in its nakedness, when it sees itself clearly.

Eryximachus

It is most true that if our soul purges itself of all falseness, and deprives itself of every fraudulent addition to *what is*, our existence is at once endangered by this cold, exact, reasonable, and moderate consideration of human life as it is.

Phaedrus

Life blackens on contact with truth, as does the dubious mushroom—when crushed—on contact with the air.

Socrates

Eryximachus, I was asking you if there were a remedy?

Eryximachus

Why cure so reasonable an ill? No doubt there is nothing more morbid in itself, nothing more inimical to nature, than *to see things as they are*. A cold and perfect clarity is a poison impossible to combat. The real, in its pure state, stops the heart instantaneously. . . . One drop of that icy lymph suffices to relax in a soul the springs and palpitations of desire, exterminate all hopes, ruin all the gods present in our blood. The Virtues and the most noble colors pale before it, and are little by little consumed. To a handful of ashes is the past reduced, and the future to a tiny icicle. The soul appears to itself as an empty and measurable form. —Here, then, things as they are come together, limit one another, and are thus chained together in the most rigorous and mortal fashion. . . . O Socrates, the universe cannot for one instant endure to be only what it is. It is strange to think that that which is All cannot be sufficient unto itself! . . . Its dismay at being what is, has therefore made it create and paint for itself a thousand masks; there is no other reason for the existence of mortals. What are mortals for? —Their business is to *know*. Know? And what is to know? —*It is assuredly: not to be what one is.* —And so here are humans raving and thinking, introducing into nature the principle of unlimited error, and myriads of marvels! . . .

The mistakes, the appearances, the play of the dioptrics of the mind deepen and quicken the world's miserable mass. . . . The idea introduces into what is, the leaven of what is not. . . . But truth sometimes shows its hand after all, and jars in the harmonious system of phantasmagorias and errors. . . . Everything threatens to perish forthwith, and Socrates comes in person to ask of me a remedy for this desperate case of clear-sightedness and tedium! . . .

Socrates

Well, Eryximachus, since there is no cure, can you tell me, at least, what state is the most contrary to this horrible state of pure disgust, of murderous lucidity, and of inexorable clarity?

Eryximachus

In the first place I see all the madnesses that are not melancholic.

Socrates

And then?

Eryximachus

Drunkenness, and the category of illusions due to heady vapors.

Socrates

Yes. But are there no kinds of intoxication which have not their source in wine?

Eryximachus

Assuredly. Love, hate, greed intoxicate! . . . And the sense of power. . . .

Socrates

All this gives taste and color to life. But the chance of hating, or of loving, or of acquiring very great possessions is bound up with all the hazards of the real. . . . Do you not see then, Eryximachus, that among all intoxications the noblest, the one most inimical to that great tedium, is the intoxication due to acts? Our acts, and more particularly those of our acts which set our bodies in motion, may bring us into a strange and admirable state. . . . It is the state farthest removed from that wretched state in which we left the motionless and lucid observer we were imagining just now.

Phaedrus

But if, by some miracle, this observer were seized with a sudden passion for dance? . . . If he wished to cease being clear in order to become light; and if then, essaying his skill at differing infinitely from himself, he tried to change his freedom of judgment into freedom of movement?

Socrates

In that case, he would teach us, at one stroke, what we are now trying to elucidate. . . . But there is something yet which I must ask Eryximachus.

Eryximachus

What you will, dear Socrates.

Socrates

Tell me then, wise physician, who hast fathomed in thy studies and circumnavigations the science of all living things; deeply versed as thou art in the forms and freaks of nature, and renowned for the classification of remarkable beasts and plants (the harmful and benign; the anodyne and the efficacious; the surprising, the frightful, the ridiculous; the dubious; and finally those that do not exist)—say then, hast thou never heard tell of those strange animals that live and flourish in the very flame itself?

Eryximachus

Assuredly! . . . Their shape and habits, dear Socrates, have been well studied—although their very existence has been recently a matter of contestation. I have very often described them to my disciples; yet I have never had the opportunity of observing any with my own eyes.

Socrates

Well then, does it not seem to you, Eryximachus, and to you, my dear Phaedrus, that that creature that is quivering over there, fluttering adorably within our gaze, that ardent Athikte, who divides and gathers herself together again, who rises and falls, so promptly opening out and closing in, and who appears to belong to constellations other than ours—seems to live, completely at ease, in an element comparable to fire—in a most subtle essence of music and movement, wherein she breathes boundless energy, while she participates with all her being in the pure and immediate violence of extreme felicity? —If we compare our grave and weighty condition with the state of that sparkling salamander, does it not seem to you that our ordinary acts, begotten by our successive needs, and our gestures and incidental movements are like coarse materials, like an impure stuff of duration—whilst that exaltation and that vibration of life, that supremacy of tension, that transport into the highest agility one is capable of, have the virtues and the potencies of flame; and that the shames, the worries, the sillinesses, and the monotonous foods of existence are consumed within it, making what is divine in a mortal woman shine before our eyes?

Phaedrus

Admirable Socrates, look quickly: how truly you

55

speak! . . . Look at the palpitating one! Dance seems to issue from her body like a flame!

Socrates

O Flame! . . .

—Perhaps this girl is a fool? . . .

O Flame! . . .

—And who can tell what superstitions and idle talk make up her soul of every day?

O Flame, notwithstanding! . . . Thing live and divine! . . .

But what is a flame, O my friends, if not *the moment itself*? —What is wild and joyful and formidable in the instant itself! . . . Flame is the act of that moment which is between earth and heaven. O my friends, all that passes from the heavy state to the subtle state passes through the moment of fire and light. . . .

And flame, is it not also the proud, ungraspable form assumed by the noblest destruction? —What will never happen again happens magnificently before our eyes! —What will never happen again must happen in the most magnificent manner possible! —As the voice recklessly sings, as the flame sings wildly between matter and ether— and from matter to ether, roars and rushes furiously—is not the great Dance, O my friends, that deliverance of our body entirely possessed by the spirit of falsehood, and of music which is falsehood, and drunk with the denial of null reality? —Look at that body, which leaps as flame replaces flame, look how it spurns and betramples what is true! How it furiously, joyously destroys the very place upon which it is, and how it intoxicates itself with the excess of its changes!

But how it wrestles with the spirit! See you not that it would vie in speed and variety with its own soul? It is strangely jealous of that freedom and ubiquity which it thinks the mind possesses! . . .

Without doubt the unique and perpetual object of the soul is that which does not exist: that which was and no longer is; that which will be and is not yet; that which is possible, and impossible—all that is the soul's concern, but never, *never* that which is!

And the body, which is that which is: see it here unable to contain itself in extension! —Where is it to put itself? —Where become? —This *One* wishes to play at being *All*. It wishes to play at the universality of the soul! It wishes to atone for its identity by the number of its acts! Being a thing, it bursts into events! —It is transported! —And just as thought, when stirred, touches all substances, vibrates between time-beat and instant, o'erleaps all differences; and just as in our minds hypotheses take shape symmetrically and possibles line up and are counted—so this body exercises itself in all its parts, joins in with itself, assumes shape upon shape, and goes out of itself incessantly! . . . At last we have it here in that state comparable to flame, in the midst of the most active exchanges. . . . We can no longer speak of "movement" . . . nor distinguish any longer its acts from its limbs. . . .

That woman who was there is being devoured by innumerable figures. . . . That body, in its bursts of vigor, offers me an extreme thought: even as we demand of our soul many things for which it was not made, and require of it to illumine us, to prophesy, to divine the future, adjuring it even to discover the God—even so the body which is there wishes to attain to an entire possession of itself, and to a point of glory that is supernatural. . . . But our body fares as does the soul, for which the God, and the wisdom, and the depth demanded of it are, and can only be, moments,

57

flashes, fragments of an alien time, desperate leaps out of its form. . . .

Phaedrus

Look, only look! . . . She is dancing yonder and gives to the eyes what here you are trying to tell us. . . . She makes the instant to be seen. . . . Through what jewels she passes! . . . She flings her gestures like scintillations! . . . She filches from nature impossible attitudes, even under the very eye of Time! . . . And Time lets himself be fooled. . . . She passes through the absurd with impunity. . . . She is divine in the Unstable, offers it as a gift to our regard! . . .

Eryximachus

Instant engenders form, and form makes the instant visible.

Phaedrus

She flees her shadow up into the air!

Socrates

We never see her but about to fall. . . .

Eryximachus

She has made all her body as smooth, as well-knit as an agile hand. . . . Only my hand can imitate that possession and ease in all her body. . . .

Socrates

O my friends, do you not feel yourselves shaken into intoxication by fits and starts, and as though by blows repeated ever more vigorously, gradually made into the likeness of all these guests, stamping and no longer able to keep their daemons silent and hidden? I feel myself invaded by extraordinary forces. . . . Or I feel that they are going forth from me, ignorant though I was that these virtues were mine. In a sonorous world, resonant and rebounding, this intense festival of the body in the presence of our souls offers light and joy. . . . All is more solemn, all more light, all more lively, all stronger; all is possible in another way; all can begin again indefinitely. . . . Nothing can resist the alternation of the strong beat with the weak. . . . Beat on, beat on! . . . Matter struck and beaten, clashing in cadence; earth well-beaten; skins and strings well-stretched, well-beaten; palms of hands, heels, striking well, beating time, forging joy and folly; and all things, caught in this rhythm of delirium, hold sway.

But joy, increasing and rebounding, tends to outbrim all measure, shakes with the blows of a battering-ram the walls which keep being from being. Men and women in cadence lead the song on to tumult. All beat and sing at once, and something grows greater and higher. . . . I hear the clash of all the glittering arms of life! . . . The cymbals crush in our ears any utterance of secret thoughts. They resound like kisses from lips of bronze. . . .

Eryximachus

Athikte, meanwhile, presents one last figure. All her body on the might of that big toe moves.

Phaedrus

Her toe, which sustains her entirely, like thumb on drumskin drums along the ground. What attention there is in that toe; what will stiffens it and maintains it on its tip! . . . But see her now, turning, twirling round herself. . . .

59

Socrates

She turns round herself—and see how things eternally linked begin to separate out. She turns and turns. . . .

Eryximachus

This is truly to penetrate into another world. . . .

Socrates

This is the supreme essay. . . . She turns, and all that is visible detaches itself from her soul; all the slime of her soul is separated at the last from its most pure; men and things will form around her a shapeless whirl of lees. . . .

See. . . . She turns. . . . A body, by its simple force, and its act, is powerful enough to alter the nature of things more profoundly than ever the mind in its speculations and dreams was able to do!

Phaedrus

One would think this could last forever.

Socrates

She could die, thus. . . .

Eryximachus

Sleep, perhaps—fall into a magic slumber. . . .

Socrates

She would rest motionless in the very center of her movement. Alone, alone to herself, like the axis of the world. . . .

Phaedrus

She turns, she turns. . . . She is falling!

Socrates

She has fallen!

Phaedrus

She is dead. . . .

Socrates

She has exhausted her second reserve of strength, and the innermost hidden treasure of her frame!

Phaedrus

Gods! She may die. . . . Eryximachus, go!

Eryximachus

I do not hurry in such circumstances! If things are to come right, it is proper that the physician should not disturb them, and should arrive a very short moment before the recovery, keeping pace with the Gods.

Socrates

But we must go and see.

Phaedrus

How white she is!

Eryximachus

Let rest act to cure her of her movement.

Phaedrus

You think she is not dead?

Eryximachus

Look at this tiny breast, asking only to live. See how faintly it pulses, clinging to time. . . .

Phaedrus

I see it only too well.

Eryximachus

The bird flutters its wings a little before taking to flight again.

Socrates

She seems happy enough.

Phaedrus

What did she say?

Socrates

She said something for herself alone.

Eryximachus

She said: "How well I feel!"

Phaedrus

The little heap of limbs and scarves is stirring. . . .

Eryximachus

Come, child, shall we open our eyes? How do you feel now?

Athikte

I feel nothing. I am not dead. And yet, I am not alive!

Socrates

Whence do you return?

Athikte

Refuge, refuge, O my refuge, O Whirlwind! I was in thee, O movement—outside all things. . . .

EUPALINOS,

OR

The Architect

πρὸς χάριν

Phaedrus

What are you doing here, Socrates? I have been seeking you this long time past. I have made my way through our dim habitation, I have asked for you everywhere. Everyone here knows you, and yet no one had seen you. Why did you withdraw from the other shades, and what thought has collected your soul apart from ours, on the frontiers of this transparent realm?

Socrates

Wait. I cannot answer. You know well that reflection among the dead is indivisible. We are now too much simplified not to undergo to its very end the motion of some idea. The living have a body which permits them to go out from knowledge and to enter into it again. They are like a house and a bee.

Phaedrus

Wonderful Socrates, I hold my peace.

Socrates

I thank you for your silence. By observing it, you make to the gods and to my thought the hardest of sacrifices. You have consumed your curiosity, and offered up your impatience to my soul. Speak freely now, and if there remains in you some desire to question me, I am ready to reply, now that I have finished with questioning myself and replying to myself. —But it is rare that a question that we have repressed is not instantly swallowed up.

Phaedrus

Then why this exile? What are you doing, separated from us all? Alcibiades, Zeno, Menexenus, Lysis, all our friends are surprised not to see you. They speak aimlessly, and their shades drone on.

Socrates

Look and hear.

Phaedrus

I hear nothing. I see very little.

Socrates

Perhaps you are not sufficiently dead. Here is the limit of our domain. Before you flows a river.

Phaedrus

Alas! Poor Ilissus!

Socrates

This river is the river of Time. It casts only the souls upon this bank; but it carries away everything else without effort.

Phaedrus

I begin to see something. But I can make nothing out. For an instant my gaze follows all that passes and drifts by, which it then loses without having divided it. . . . If I were not dead, this movement would nauseate me—so sad is it and irresistible. Or else I should be constrained to imitate it, as human bodies do; I should fall asleep in order to flow away myself.

Socrates

Yet this great flux is made of all such things as you have known or might have known. This vast irregular sheet of water, which rushes by without respite, rolls all colors towards nothingness. See how dim it all is.

Phaedrus

Every instant I imagine that I am going to discern some form, but what I think I have seen never succeeds in awakening the least image in my mind.

Socrates

That is because you are witnessing the true flow of beings, motionless yourself in death. We see, from this pure bank, all human things and natural forms impelled in accordance with the true speed of their essence. We are like the dreamer, in whose breast, shapes and thoughts being strangely altered by their flight, things and their transformations intermingle and are blent. Here everything is negligible, yet everything counts. Crimes engender immense benefits, and the greatest virtues develop fatal consequences: our judgment settles on nothing, idea becomes sensation before our very eyes, and every man drags after him a chain of monsters inextricably wrought of his acts and the successive forms of his body. I think of the presence and of the habits of mortals in this so fluid stream, and reflect that I was one among them, striving to see all things just as I see them at this very moment. I then placed Wisdom in the eternal station which now is ours. But from here all is unrecognizable. Truth is before us, and we no longer understand anything at all.

Phaedrus

But whence, O Socrates, can proceed that bent for the eternal which is sometimes to be noticed among the living? You pursued knowledge. Men of the grosser sort try desperately to preserve the very bodies of the dead. Others build temples and tombs which they strive to render indestructible. The wisest and best inspired of men wish to give to their thoughts a harmony and a cadence which shall guard them against change and oblivion.

Socrates

You see clearly, O Phaedrus, what folly it is! But the Fates have decreed that among the things indispensable to the race of men, there must figure some insensate desires. There would be no men without love. Nor would science exist without absurd ambitions. And whence, think you, have we drawn the primal idea and the energy for those immense efforts which have raised so many illustrious cities and useless monuments which reason admires, though she would have been incapable of conceiving them?

Phaedrus

But reason had yet some part in the matter. All, without her, would be level with the earth.

Socrates

All.

Phaedrus

Do you remember those constructions that we saw building at the Piraeus?

Socrates

Yes.

Phaedrus

Do you recall those engines, those efforts, tempered by the music of flutes; those operations so exact, that progress at once so mysterious and so clear? What confusion at the first, melting, as it seemed, into order! What solidity, what rigor were engendered between those plumb lines, and along those frail cords stretched so as to be just breasted by the growing layers of brick!

Socrates

I preserve that fine memory. O materials! Beautiful stones! . . . O how light are we become!

Phaedrus

And that temple outside the walls, near the altar of Boreas—do you remember?

Socrates

The temple of Artemis the Huntress?

Phaedrus

The very one. One day we were out there. We were discoursing of Beauty. . . .

Socrates

Alas!

Phaedrus

I was a close friend of him who built that temple. He came from Megara and was called Eupalinos. He gladly

69

spoke to me of his art, of all the care and the knowledge that it requires; he made me understand everything that I saw with him in his workshop. I observed, above all, his astounding mind. I found in him the power of Orpheus. He foretold their monumental future to the shapeless heaps of stones and beams that lay around us; and those materials, at his voice, seemed dedicated to the one and only place to which the fates propitious to the goddess would have assigned them. How wonderful were his instructions to the workmen! They retained no trace of his difficult meditations of the night before. He gave them nothing but commands and figures.

Socrates

That is the very way of God.

Phaedrus

His instructions and their acts fitted together so happily that it seemed as though these men were nothing more nor less than his limbs. You cannot believe, Socrates, what a joy it was for my soul to have knowledge of a thing so well regulated. I no longer separate the idea of a temple from that of its edification. When I see one, I see an admirable action, yet more glorious than a victory and more contrary to wretched nature. Destroying and constructing are equal in importance, and we must have souls for the one and the other; but constructing is the dearer to my mind. O most happy Eupalinos!

Socrates

What enthusiasm of a shade for a phantom! —I did not know this Eupalinos. Was he, then, a great man? I perceive that he rose to the supreme knowledge of his art. Is he here?

Phaedrus

Doubtless he is amongst us; but I have never yet met him in this land.

Socrates

I know not what he could build here. Here the very projects are memories. But reduced as we are to the sole pleasures of conversation, I should be glad to listen to him.

Phaedrus

I have retained some of his precepts. I scarcely know if they would please you. They certainly enchant me.

Socrates

Can you repeat me any one of them?

Phaedrus

Well, listen. He used very often to say: "There are no details in execution."

Socrates

I understand and do not understand. I understand something, and I am not sure that it is really what he meant.

Phaedrus

And I am certain that your subtle wit has not failed to catch his meaning. In a soul as clear and as complete as yours, it must come to pass that a craftsman's maxim assumes a force and range entirely new. If it be truly perspicuous, and drawn directly from the work by a swift act of the mind that sums up its experience, without giving itself time to go astray, such a maxim is precious matter for the philosopher; it is an ingot of raw gold that I hand to you, goldsmith!

Socrates

I was the goldsmith of my chains!—But let us consider this precept. The eternity we have here invites us not to be niggardly of words. This infinite duration either must not *be*, or must contain all possible discourses, the true as well as the false. I can therefore speak without any fear of being in error; for if I am in error now, I shall presently say what is true, and if I am saying what is true, I shall say what is false a little later on.

O Phaedrus, you have surely not failed to notice in the most important speeches, whether the matter be politics or the private interests of citizens, or again in the delicate language that a lover has to use at some decisive moment—you have certainly noticed what weight and what significance are assumed by the very least of little words, and the smallest of silences that falls between them. And I, who have spoken so much, with the insatiable desire to convince, have convinced myself in the long run that the weightiest arguments and the best-conducted demonstrations would have had mighty little effect, but for the help of these apparently insignificant details; and that, on the other hand, mediocre reasons, fittingly linked to words full of tact, or gilded like crowns, can seduce the ears for long. These go-betweens are at the portals of the mind. They tell it what they please, and repeat it at pleasure, finally making the mind believe that it hears its own voice. The reality of a speech is after all that melody and that coloring of a voice which we wrongly treat as details and accidents.

Phaedrus

You are making an immense detour, dear Socrates, but I see you returning from so far away, with a thousand other examples, and all your dialectical forces in array!

Socrates

Consider also the art of the surgeon. The most skillful operator in the world, who puts his busy fingers into your wound, be his hands never so light, so experienced, so discerning; however surely he feel the position of the organs and the veins, their interrelation and their depth; however great be his certitude about the acts which he intends to accomplish in your flesh, about the things to be cut away and the things to be reunited; if through a circumstance that has escaped his attention, some thread, some needle he is using, some nothing that is of use for his operation, be not strictly pure, or sufficiently purified, he kills you. You are dead. . . .

Phaedrus

Fortunately the thing is done! That is precisely what happened to me.

Socrates

You are dead, I say, you are dead, cured according to all the rules; for, once all the demands of art and those of the moment have been complied with, thought lovingly contemplates her work. —But you are dead. A strand of ill-prepared silk has made science a murderess; this slightest of details has brought to nothing the work of Aesculapius and Athena.

Phaedrus

Eupalinos knew that well.

Socrates

It is so in all domains, excepting that of the philosophers, whose great misfortune it is that they never see the universes they imagine collapse, since they do not exist.

73

Phaedrus

Eupalinos was the man of his precept. He neglected nothing. He ordered small laths to be cut following the grain of the wood, so that, when placed between the masonry and the beams which rested thereon, they should prevent the damp from rising into the fiber and rotting it when once absorbed. He gave a like care to all the sensitive points of the building. You would have thought that it was his own body he was tending. During the process of construction he scarcely left the works. I truly believe that he knew every stone in the place. He saw to the precision of their cutting; he minutely studied all the means that have been thought of for preventing the edges from being injured and the exactness of the joining from being impaired. He directed carvings to be contrived, toothings to be left, sloping edges to be made in the marble facings. He took the most exquisite pains with the coatings of polish which he ordered to be spread over the walls of plain stone.

But all these delicate devices making for the permanence of the edifice were as nothing to those which he employed when he elaborated the emotions and vibrations of the soul of the future beholder of his work.

For the light he prepared a matchless instrument, which would redistribute it, endowing it with intelligible forms and almost musical properties, into the space where mortals move. Like those orators and poets you had in mind just now, he knew, O Socrates, the mysterious virtue of imperceptible modulations. None perceived, when confronted by a mass so delicately lightened and so simple of aspect, that he was being led to a sort of bliss by insensible curves, by minute and all-powerful inflections; and by those deep-wrought combinations of the regular and the irregular which he had introduced and concealed, and made as imperious as they were indefinable. They caused the ever-shifting spectator, obedient to their invisible presence, to pass from vision to vision, and from great spells of silence to mutterings of delight, according as he advanced, retreated, approached again, and as he moved within the radius of the work, impelled by its influence, and the plaything of admiration alone. "My temple," this man from Megara would say, "must move men as they are moved by their beloved."

Socrates

That is divine. I once heard, dear Phaedrus, an expression quite similar, and quite the contrary. One of our friends, whom it is useless to name, said of our Alcibiades who was so beautifully made: "Looking at him, one feels oneself becoming an architect! . . ." How I pity you, dear Phaedrus! You are much more unhappy here than I. I cared for the True alone; I gave my life to it. Well, in these Elysian meadows, though I still wonder if I have not made a rather sorry bargain, I can still imagine that there remains something for me to know. I gladly seek among the shades, the shade of some truth. But you, whose desires were formed and whose acts were governed by Beauty alone, are left resourceless here. Bodies are memories, faces are smoke; so also with this light so uniform at every point; so feeble and so sickening in its paleness; this general indifference which it illumines, or rather which it impregnates, without sketching out anything sharply; these half-transparent groups which we form with our ghosts; these deadened voices which scarce remain to us and which sound as though they were whispered into the thickness of a fleece or into the indolence of a fog. . . . You must be suffering, dear Phaedrus! And yet not be suffering enough. . . . Even that is forbidden us, since to suffer is to be alive.

Phaedrus

Every instant I think I am going to suffer. . . . But do not speak, I beseech you, of what I have lost. Leave my memory to itself. Leave to it its sun and its statues! O what a contrast takes possession of me! There is perhaps for memories a sort of second death which I have not yet suffered. But I live again, I see once more the ephemeral skies! What is most beautiful finds no place in the eternal!

Socrates

Where, then, do you place it?

Phaedrus

Nothing beautiful is separable from life, and life is that which dies.

Socrates

So we may say. . . . But most people have of Beauty an immortal notion of some kind.

Phaedrus

I tell you, Socrates, that Beauty, according to the Phaedrus I was . . .

Socrates

Is Plato not in these parts?

Phaedrus

I am speaking against him.

Socrates

Well, speak!

Phaedrus

. . . does not reside in certain rare objects, nor even in those models situate outside nature, and contemplated by the noblest souls as the exemplars of their designs and the secret types to which their works would conform; sacred things, which should be spoken of in the very words of the poet: *Gloire du long désir, Idées!*

Socrates

What poet?

Phaedrus

The very admirable Stephanos, who appeared so many centuries after us. But to my mind, the idea of these Ideas, of which our wonderful Plato is the father, is infinitely too simple, and as it were too pure, to explain the diversity of Beauties, the change of preferences in men, the effacement of so many works that were cried up to the skies, the completely new creations, and the resurrections which it is impossible to foresee. And there are many other objections!

Socrates

But what is your own thought?

Phaedrus

I no longer know how to grasp it. Nothing contains, everything implies it. It is within me, like my own self; it acts infallibly; it judges, it desires. . . . But as for expressing it, I find it as difficult as saying what makes me to be myself, a thing that I know so precisely and yet so little.

Socrates

But since the gods, dear Phaedrus, allow our conversation to continue in these lower regions, where we have forgotten nothing, where we have learnt something, where we find ourselves placed beyond everything human, we must now know what is truly beautiful, what is ugly; what befits man; what can fill him with wonder without confounding him, possess him without stupefying him. . . .

Phaedrus

It is that which puts him, without effort, above his own nature.

Socrates

"Without effort?" "Above his nature?"

Phaedrus

Yes.

Socrates

"Without effort?" How is that possible? "Above his nature?" What does this mean? I inevitably picture a man trying to climb up on his own shoulders! . . . Repelled by this absurd image, I ask, Phaedrus, how can one cease to be oneself, and then return to one's essence? And how can this take place without violence?

I well know that the extremes of love, and excess of wine, or again the astounding effect of those vapors that the Pythia breathes in, take us, as the saying goes, out of ourselves; and I know even better, by my very certain experience, that our souls can, in the very heart of time, make for themselves sanctuaries impenetrable to duration, eternal in their inner selves, but transient with regard to nature; where they at last are what they know; where they desire what they are; where they feel themselves to be created by what they love, and render back to it light for light, and silence for silence, giving themselves and receiving themselves again without borrowing aught from the stuff the world is made of, nor from the Hours. They are then like those sparkling calms, circumscribed by tempests, which shift from place to place on the seas. What are we during these abysses? They imply the life they suspend. . . .

But these marvels, these spells of contemplation, these ecstasies do not illuminate for me our strange problem of beauty. I am unable to connect these supreme states of the soul with the presence of a body or of some object which brings them into being.

Phaedrus

O Socrates, it is because you always wish to draw everything out of yourself! . . . You, whom of all men I admire, you, more beautiful in your life, more beautiful in your death, than the most beautiful of visible things; great Socrates, adorable ugliness, all-powerful Thought that changest poison into an elixir of immortality, O thou who, grown cold, and the half of thy body already marble, the other still vocal, didst speak to us lovingly in the language of a god, let me tell thee what thing was perhaps wanting in thy experience.

Socrates

It is somewhat late to acquaint me with it now. But speak all the same.

Phaedrus

One thing, Socrates, one single thing you lacked. You were a divine man, and you had perhaps no need of the material beauties of the world. You scarce tasted of them. You did not, I know, disdain the sweetness of the country-side, the splendor of the city, nor yet the freshness of spring water, nor the delicate shade of the plane tree; but they were for you merely the distant ornaments of your meditations, the delightful environment of your doubtings, a favorable site for your inward steps. And as what was most beautiful would lead you far away from itself, you were always seeing something else.

Socrates

Man, and the mind of man.

Phaedrus

But still, did you never meet among men some whose singular passion for forms and appearances surprised you?

Socrates

No doubt.

Phaedrus

And yet whose intelligence and virtues were inferior to none?

Socrates

To be sure I did!

Phaedrus

Did you place them higher or lower than the philosophers?

Socrates

That depends.

Phaedrus

Did their object seem to you more or less worthy of search and of love than your own?

Socrates

It is not a question of their object. I cannot think that
there exists more than one Sovereign Good. But what remains obscure to me and difficult to understand is that men
so pure, as regards their intelligence, should have need of
sensible forms and bodily graces to attain their highest state.

Phaedrus

One day, dear Socrates, I spoke of this very thing with
my friend Eupalinos.

"Phaedrus," he was saying to me, "the more I meditate
on my art, the more I practice it; the more I think and act,
the more I suffer and rejoice as an architect—and the more
I feel my own being with an ever surer delight and clarity.

"I lose myself in long spells of expectation; I find myself
again by the surprises I give myself; by means of the successive steps of my silence, I advance in my own edification;
and I approach to such an exact correspondence between my
aims and my powers, that I seem to myself to have made of
the existence that was given me a sort of human handiwork.

"By dint of constructing," he put it with a smile, "I truly
believe that I have constructed myself."

Socrates

To construct oneself, to know oneself—are these two
distinct acts or not?

Phaedrus

. . . and he added: "I have sought accuracy in my
thoughts, so that, being clearly engendered by the consideration of things, they might be changed as though of
their own accord into the acts of my art. I have apportioned
my attentions; I have arranged the problems in another

81

order; I begin where I finished off formerly, so as to go a little further. . . . I am niggardly of musings, I conceive as though I were executing. No more now, in the shapeless void of my soul, do I contemplate those imaginary edifices, which are to real edifices what chimeras and gorgons are to true animals. But what I think, is feasible, and what I do, is related to the intelligible. . . . And then. . . . Listen, Phaedrus," he went on to say, "that little temple, which I built for Hermes, a few steps from here, if you could know what it means to me! —There where the passer-by sees but an elegant chapel—'t is but a trifle: four columns, a very simple style— there I have enshrined the memory of a bright day in my life. O sweet metamorphosis! This delicate temple, none knows it, is the mathematical image of a girl of Corinth, whom I happily loved. It reproduces faithfully the proportions that were peculiarly hers. It lives for me! It gives me back what I have given it. . . . "

"That then is why it is of an inexplicable grace," I said to him. "One does indeed feel the presence of a person, the first flower of a woman, the harmony of a charming being. It vaguely awakens a memory which cannot reach its goal; and this beginning of an image of which you possess the perfection, does not fail to incite and confound the soul. Do you know, if I give myself up to my thought, I shall be comparing it to some nuptial song intermingled with flutes, which I feel coming to birth in me."

Eupalinos looked at me with a more definite and more tender friendliness.

"Oh!" said he, "how you seem made to understand me! None has come closer than you to my daemon. I would willingly confide all my secrets to you; but of some I myself could not speak adequately, for they defy language; the others would run a great chance of wearying you, for they are connected with the most special processes and the most detailed knowledge of my art. I can only tell you what truths, if not what mysteries, you were just now hinting at, when you spoke to me of concert, song, and flutes, in reference to my young temple. Tell me (since you are so sensible to the effects of architecture), have you not noticed, in walking about this city, that among the buildings with which it is peopled, certain are *mute*; others *speak*; and others, finally—and they are the most rare—*sing?*—It is not their purpose, nor even their general features, that give them such animation, or that reduce them to silence. These things depend upon the talent of their builder, or on the favor of the Muses."

"Now that you point it out, I notice this was already in my mind."

"Good. Those among buildings that neither speak nor sing deserve only scorn; they are dead things, lower in the hierarchy than the heaps of rubble vomited by contractors' carts, which at least amuse the sagacious eye by the accidental order they borrow from their fall. . . . As for the monuments that limit themselves to speech, if they speak clearly, I esteem them. Here, say they, the tradesmen meet. Here the judges deliberate. Here captives groan. Here the lovers of debauchery. . . . (I then told Eupalinos that I had seen very remarkable buildings in this last style. But he did not hear me.) These markets, these tribunals, and these prisons, when those that build them know their business, speak the most definite language. The one kind visibly draw in an active and ever-changing crowd; they offer it peristyles and porticoes; by means of their many doors and easy flights of steps they invite all to enter their vast, well-lighted halls, to form groups, to give themselves up to the ferment of business. . . . But the habitations of justice should speak to

83

the eye of the rigor and equity of our laws. Majesty befits them, masses completely bare; and an awe-inspiring amplitude of wall. The silences of those bleak surfaces are scarce broken, at far intervals, by the threat of a mysterious door, or by the grim gesture of the thick iron bars against the gloom of the narrow window they guard. All here pronounces sentence—everything is eloquent of penalties. The stone gravely declares that which it shuts in; the wall is implacable, and this work of stone, conforming so closely to the truth, strongly proclaims its stern purpose. . . ."

Socrates

My prison was not so terrible. . . . If I recollect, it was a drab and indifferent place in itself.

Phaedrus

How can you say so!

Socrates

I confess that I gave it little thought. I saw only my friends, immortality, and death.

Phaedrus

And I was not with you!

Socrates

Plato was not either, nor Aristippus. . . . But the room was full, the walls were hidden from me. The evening light cast flesh tints on the stones of the vault. . . . In truth, dear Phaedrus, I never had a prison other than my body. But come back to what your friend said to you. I think he was going to speak of the most precious edifices, and I should like to hear about them.

Phaedrus

Well, I will continue.

Eupalinos went on to give me a magnificent picture of those gigantic constructions which we admire in ports. They advance into the sea. Their arms, of a hard, absolute whiteness, circumscribe the lulled docks whose calm they defend. They keep them in security, peacefully gorged with galleys, sheltered by the bristling breakwaters and the resounding piers. High towers, where someone keeps watch, where during impenetrable nights the flame of pine cones dances and rages, command the offing at the foaming extremities of the moles. . . . To venture upon such works is to brave Neptune himself. You must fling mountains by the cartload into the waters you wish to enclose. You must pit the coarse rubble drawn from the depths of the earth against the shifting depths of the sea, and against the monotonous onslaught of the riders, urged on by the wind as it sweeps by. . . . Those ports, those vast ports, said my friend, what a sudden brightness in the mind! How they develop their several parts! How they descend to their task!—But the wonders peculiar to the sea, and the accidental statuary of the shores are given to the architect by a grace of the gods. All conspires towards the effect produced on our souls by these noble, half-natural constructions: the presence of the pure horizon, the waxing and the waning of a sail, the emotion that comes of being severed from the earth, the beginning of perils, the sparkling threshold of lands unknown; and the very eagerness of the men, ready as it is to change into a superstitious dread the moment they give in to it and set foot aboard. . . . Admirable theaters they are, in truth; but let us place above them the edifices of art alone! It is necessary to abstract oneself from the spells of life and from immediate enjoyment, even if for this purpose we must make a stern effort against ourselves. What is most beautiful is of necessity tyrannical. . . .

But I said to Eupalinos that I did not see why this must be so. He replied that true beauty is precisely as rare as is, among men, the man capable of making an effort against himself, that is to say, of choosing a certain self and of imposing it upon himself. And then, taking up again the golden thread of his thought: "I now come," said he, "to the master-pieces entirely due to someone, of which I said, a moment ago, that they seem to sing of themselves.

"Was that a vain saying, O Phaedrus? Were these mere words negligently engendered by the discourse they adorn as it goes rapidly on its way, but which do not bear pondering over? No, Phaedrus, most assuredly no! . . . And when, first of us two and without special intent, you spoke of music with reference to my temple, you were visited by a divine analogy. That hymen of thoughts which was consummated on your lips, as the unreflecting act of your voice; that seemingly fortuitous union of things so different, comes of an admirable necessity, which it is almost impossible to conceive in all its profundity, but whose persuasive presence you have obscurely felt. Just imagine strongly what would be the nature of a mortal pure enough, reasonable enough, subtle and tenacious enough, powerfully enough armed by Minerva to think out to the ultimate limits of his being, and therefore to ultimate reality, that strange parallel of visible forms with the ephemeral combinations of successive sounds; think . . . towards what an intimate and universal origin he would advance; what a precious point of vantage he would reach; what a god he would find in his own flesh! And possessing himself finally in this state of divine am-biguity, if he then proposed to build I know not what monuments, whose gracious and venerable features should partake directly of the purity of musical sound, or were designed to communicate to the soul the emotion coming of an inexhaustible accord—think, Phaedrus, what a man! Imagine what edifices! . . . And for us what delights!"

"And do you," I said to him, "conceive this?"

"Yes and no. Yes, as a dream. No, as a science."

"Do you draw some help from these thoughts?"

"Yes, as an incentive. Yes, as a verdict. Yes, as a punishment. . . . But it is not in my power to link up, as I ought, an analysis with an ecstasy. Sometimes I come near to this precious power. . . . Once I was infinitely near to seizing it, but only in the way one possesses during sleep an object beloved. I can only speak to you of the approaches towards so great a thing. When it makes its presence known, dear Phaedrus, I am already as different from myself as a tightened string differs from itself when loose and sinuous. I am quite other than what I am. All is clear and seems easy. Then my schemes follow their own course and are preserved in a light that is mine. I feel my need of beauty, proportionate to my unknown resources, engendering of itself alone forms that give it satisfaction. I desire with my whole being. . . . The powers assemble. The powers of the soul, as you know, come strangely up out of the night. . . . By force of illusion they advance to the very borders of the real. I summon them, I adjure them by my silence. . . . Here they come, charged with clarity and with error. The true, the false shine equally in their eyes, on their diadems. They crush me with their gifts, they besiege me with their wings. . . . Phaedrus, here lies the peril! It is the most difficult thing in the world! . . . O moment most important of all! O chiefest rending! . . . These mysterious and overbountiful favors, far from welcoming them as they are, solely derived from the great desire and naïvely formed of the extreme expectation of my soul, I must arrest them, O Phaedrus, and they must await my signal. And having obtained them by a sort of interruption of my life (an adorable suspension of ordinary duration), I still force myself to divide the indivisible, and to temper and interrupt the very birth of Ideas. . . ."

"Poor mortal," I said to him, "what can you hope to do during a lightning flash?"

"Be free. There are many things," he resumed, "there are . . . all things in that instant; and all that busies the philosophers takes place between the glance that falls on an object and the knowledge that results . . . always ending prematurely."

"I do not understand you. Do you strive then to delay these Ideas?"

"I must. I prevent them from satisfying me, I postpone pure felicity."

"Why? Whence do you draw this cruel force?"

"What is important for me above all else is to obtain from *that which is going to be*, that it should with all the vigor of its newness satisfy the reasonable requirements of *that which has been*. How can one help being obscure? . . . Listen: one day I saw a cluster of roses and modeled it in wax. When I had finished this model, I put it in sand. Hurrying Time reduces the roses to nothing; and fire promptly returns the wax to its natural formlessness. But the wax having fled its heated mold and now being lost, the dazzling liquid of the bronze comes to wed in the hardened sand the hollow identity of the smallest petal. . . ."

"I understand! Eupalinos. This riddle is transparent to me; the myth is easy to translate.

"Do not those roses that were fresh and that perish before your eyes stand for all things about us and for moving life itself?—As for the model of wax that you made, employing upon it your deft fingers, despoiling with your eye the corollas, and returning laden with flowers to your work—is that not an image of your daily labors, enriched by the commerce between your acts and your latest observations?—The fire is Time itself, which would entirely abolish or scatter abroad into the wide world both the real roses and your roses of wax, if your being did not in some way preserve, I know not how, the forms of your experience and the secret solidity of its own reason. . . . As for the liquid bronze, it surely stands for the exceptional powers of your soul and the tumultuous state of something that wills to be born. This incandescent bounty would be dissipated in vain heat and infinite reverberations, and would leave behind nothing but ingots or irregular streaks of run metal, if you were not able to lead it by mysterious conduits to cool down and to bestow itself in the pure matrices of your wisdom. Your being must therefore of necessity divide itself and become, at one and the same instant, hot and cold, fluid and solid, free and fast—roses, wax, and fire; matrix and Corinthian metal."

"Exactly! But I told you that I merely try my hand at it."

"How do you set about it?"

"As best I can."

"But tell me how you try."

"Listen once more then, since you will it so. . . . I cannot very well make clear for you what is not clear for myself. . . . O Phaedrus, when I design a dwelling (whether it be for the gods, or for a man), and when I lovingly seek its form, studying to create an object that shall delight the view, that shall hold converse with the mind, that shall accord with reason and the numerous proprieties . . . I confess, how strange soever it may appear to you, *that it seems to me my body is playing its part in the game*. . . . Let me explain. This

body is an admirable instrument, of which I am sure that
those who are alive and who all have it at their disposal do
not make full use. They draw from it only pleasure, pain,
and indispensable acts, such as living. Sometimes they become identical with it; sometimes again they forget its
existence for a space; and, at one moment mere brutes, at
another pure spirits, they know not what multitudinous
bonds with all things they have in themselves, and of what
a marvelous substance they are made. And yet it is through
this substance that they participate in what they see and what
they touch: they are stones, they are trees; they exchange
contacts and breaths with the matter that englobes them.
They touch, they are touched; they have, and lift, weight;
they move, and carry their virtues and vices about; and when
they fall into a reverie or into indefinite sleep, they reproduce
the nature of waters, they turn into sand and clouds. . . . On
other occasions they store up thunderbolts and hurl them
abroad! . . .

"But their soul is unable to make exact use of that nature
which is so close to it, and which it interpenetrates. It out-
strips, it lags; it seems to flee the very instant. It receives
shocks and jolts from this body, causing it to depart into
itself, and to fade away into its own emptiness where it gives
birth to mere smoke. But I, on the contrary, the wiser for
my errors, say in the full light, I repeat to myself with every
dawn:

" 'O body of mine, that recallest to me at every moment
this tempering of my tendencies, this equilibrium of thy
organs, these true proportions of thy parts, which make thee
to *be* and to stablish thyself ever anew in the very heart of
moving things; keep watch over my work; teach me secretly the demands of nature, and impart to me that great
art, with which thou art endowed even as by it thou art

made, of surviving the seasons, and of saving thee from the
incidents of chance. Grant me to find in thy alliance the
feeling of what is true; temper, strengthen, and confirm my
thoughts. Perishable as thou art, thou art far less so than my
dreams. Thou endurest a little longer than a fancy; thou
payest for my acts, and dost expiate my errors. Instrument,
thou, of life, thou art for each one of us the sole being
which can be compared with the universe. The entire sphere
always has thee for a center; O mutual object of the attention
of all the starry heavens! Thou art indeed the measure of the
world, of which my soul presents me with the shell alone.
She knows it to be without depth, and knows it to so
little purpose that she sometimes would class it among her
dreams; she doubts the sun. . . . Doting on her ephemeral
fabrications, she thinks herself capable of an infinity of
different realities; she imagines that other worlds exist, but
thou recallest her to thyself, as the anchor calls back the
ship. . . .

" 'My intelligence, better inspired, will not, dear body,
cease henceforth to call thee to herself; nor wilt thou cease,
I trust, to furnish her with thy presences, with thy demands,
with thy local ties. For we have at last come to find, thou
and I, the means of joining ourselves, and the indissoluble
knot of our differences: to wit, a work that is our child.
We wrought each of us in his own sphere; thou by living,
and I by dreaming. My vast reveries ended in a boundless
impotence. But may this work which now I wish to make,
and which cannot be made of itself, constrain us to answer
one another, and may it spring solely from our alliance!
But this body and this mind, this presence so invincibly real
and this creative absence that strive for possession of our
being and which must finally be reconciled, this finite and
this infinite which we bring with us, each in accordance with

his nature, must now unite in a well-ordered structure; and if, thanks to the gods, they work in concert, if they interchange fitness and grace, beauty and lastingness, if they barter movements for lines, and numbers for thoughts, they will then have discovered their true relationship, their act. May they concert together, may they understand one another by means of the material of my art! Stones and forces, outlines and masses, lights and shadows, artificial groupings, the illusions of perspective and the realities of gravity, all these are the object of their commerce; and may the profit of this commerce finally be that incorruptible wealth which I name Perfection.' "

Socrates

What an unexampled prayer! . . . And what then?

Phaedrus

He was silent.

Socrates

All this rings strange in the place where we are. Now that we are deprived of our bodies, we must assuredly bewail it, and consider that life which we have left with the same envious eye with which we formerly looked on the garden of happy shades. . . . Neither our works nor our desires follow us here; but there is room for regrets.

Phaedrus

These groves are haunted by shades eternally miserable. . . .

Socrates

If I met this Eupalinos, I should ask him something further.

Phaedrus

He must feel himself the most accursed of the blest. What would you ask him?

Socrates

To explain somewhat more clearly about those buildings of which he said "that they sing."

Phaedrus

I see that phrase of his haunts you.

Socrates

There are sayings that are bees for the mind. They have the persistence of those insects that harass us. This one stung me.

Phaedrus

And what says the sting?

Socrates

It ceases not to spur me on to expatiate upon the arts. I compare them, I distinguish them; I would hear the song of the columns and visualize in the pure sky the monument of a melody. This conceit very easily leads me to set on one side Music and Architecture; and over against them, the other arts. A painting, dear Phaedrus, covers a mere surface such as a panel or a wall: and thereupon it feigns objects and personages. Statuary likewise never adorns more than a portion of our view. But a temple, along with its precincts, or again the interior of this temple, forms for us a sort of complete greatness within which we live. . . . We are, we move, we live inside the work of man! There is not a part of that triple extent that has not been studied out and reflected upon. In it we breathe in, as it were, the will and preferences of an individual. We are caught and mastered within the proportions he has chosen. We cannot escape him.

Phaedrus

No doubt.

Socrates

But do you not see that the same thing happens to us in another circumstance?

Phaedrus

What thing?

Socrates

Being inside a work of man as fishes are in the sea, being entirely immersed in it, living in it, and belonging to it?

Phaedrus

I cannot guess.

Socrates

Why, did you never experience this when present at some religious festival, or when taking part in some banquet, while the instruments filled the hall with sounds and phantoms? Did it not seem to you that an intelligible and changing space was substituted for primitive space; or, rather, that time itself surrounded you on all sides? Did you not live in a mobile edifice, incessantly renewed and reconstructed within itself, and entirely dedicated to the transformations of a soul none other than the soul of extension itself? Was there not a changing plenitude, analogous to a continuous flame, illumining and warming your whole being by an unceasing fiery consumption of memories, of forebodings, regrets, and premonitions, and of an infinity of emotions having no clear cause? And did not those moments, and their ornaments, and those dances without dancers, and those statues, bodiless and featureless (and yet so delicately outlined), seem to surround you, slave as you were of the general presence of Music? And that inexhaustible production of enchantments, were you not enclosed along with it, nay forcibly locked up, like a Pythia in her chamber of vapors?

Phaedrus

Yes, certainly. And I even have observed that to be in that enclosure and in that universe created by sounds, wherever it be, was to be outside of oneself. . . .

Socrates

And further! Have you not felt this mobility as motionless compared to your still more mobile thought? Have you not considered, at certain instants, and as though apart from yourself, that edifice of apparitions, of transitions, of conflicts, and of indefinable events, as a thing from which one can divert one's attention, and to which one can return, as by a road, to find it all nearly the same?

Phaedrus

I confess that it has happened to me to detach myself unwittingly from music, and in some sort to leave it where it was. . . . My attention strays from it, the music itself being the starting point that invites my distraction. Then I return into its bosom.

Socrates

All that mobility forms then, as it were, a solid. It seems to exist in itself, like a temple built about your soul; you can go out and away from it; you can go in again by another door. . . .

Phaedrus

That is so. And I should even say that one never goes in again by the same door.

Socrates

There are then two arts which enclose man in man; or, rather, which enclose the being in its work, and the soul in its acts and in the productions of its acts, as our former body was entirely enclosed in the creations of its eye, and surrounded with sight. By means of two arts it wraps itself up, in two different ways, in their inner laws and wills, which are figured forth in one material or another, stone or air.

Phaedrus

I well see that Music and Architecture have each of them this profound kinship with us.

Socrates

Both occupy the totality of one sense. We only escape from the one by an inner severance; from the other only by movements. And each of them fills our knowledge and our space with artificial truths, and with objects essentially human.

Phaedrus

Therefore these two arts, being so directly related to us, without intermediaries, must also have with one another a peculiarly simple relationship?

Socrates

Quite so; and you rightly say: "Without intermediaries." For the visible objects on which the other arts and poetry draw—flowers, trees, living beings (and even the immortals) —when they are employed by the artist, do not cease to be what they are, nor to mix their nature and their own significance with the design of him who uses them to express his will. Thus the painter who desires that a certain place on his picture be green, there puts a tree; and by so doing he says something more than what he wished to say initially. He adds to his work all the ideas that spring from the idea of a tree, and cannot confine himself to what suffices. He cannot separate color from some being.

Phaedrus

Such is the profit, and such the disadvantage of being enslaved to real objects; each of them is a plurality of things for man and may be turned to a plurality of different uses for his acts. . . . What you say of the painter makes me think, too, of children whom a pedagogue requires to reason upon Achilles and the tortoise, and to find out how much time a hero will need to overtake a sluggish animal. Instead of dispelling the fable from their minds, and of concentrating on the numbers and their mathematical relations, they conjure up on the one hand the winged feet, on the other the tardy tortoise; their minds enter successively into the two beings; they think the one and think the other; and creating thus two incommunicable times and spaces, never reach the state where there is no more Achilles and no more tortoise, nor even time nor speed, but numbers alone and numerical relations.

Socrates

But the arts of which we speak should, on the contrary, by means of numbers and relations of numbers, engender in us not a fable, but that hidden power which makes all fables.

These arts raise the soul to the creative pitch, and make it sonorous and fertile. The soul responds to that pure, material harmony which they communicate to her, by an inexhaustible abundance of explanations and myths which she engenders without effort; and she creates, for that invincible emotion which calculated forms and right intervals impose on her, an infinitude of imaginary causes, which make her live a thousand marvelously sudden lives that merge into one another.

Phaedrus

Neither painting nor poetry has this virtue.

Socrates

They have, it is true, virtues of their own; which, however, reside, in some sort, in the present. A beautiful body demands to be looked upon for its own sake, and offers us an admirable moment: 't is a detail of nature, which the artist has stayed by a miracle. . . . But Music and Architecture make us think of something quite other than themselves; they are in the midst of this world like the monuments of another world; or, if you will, like the examples, disseminated here and there, of a structure and duration that are not those of beings but those of forms and of laws. They seem dedicated to reminding us directly, one, of the formation of the universe, the other, of its order and stability; they invoke the constructions of the mind, and its freedom, which is in search of that order and reconstitutes it in a thousand ways; they therefore neglect the particular appearances with which the world and the mind are ordinarily occupied: plants, beasts, and people. . . . I have even observed sometimes, when listening to music, with an attention equal to its complexity, that I was as it were no longer perceiving the sounds of the instruments as sensations of the ear. The symphony itself made me forget the sense of hearing. It transformed itself so promptly, so exactly, into animated truths and universal adventures, or even into abstract combinations, that I was no longer conscious of the sensible intermediary, sound.

Phaedrus

You mean, do you not, that the statue makes one think of the statue, but that music does not make one think of music, nor a construction of another construction? That is how—if you are right—a façade can sing! But I ask myself in vain how these strange effects are possible.

Socrates

It seems to me that we have already found out.

Phaedrus

I have only got a confused notion of it.

Socrates

What did we say?—To impose upon stone or communicate to the air intelligible forms; to borrow a minimum from natural objects, to imitate as little as possible: this is common to the two arts.

Phaedrus

Yes. They have these negative qualities in common.

Socrates

But, on the other hand, to produce essentially human objects; to make use of sensible means, which yet are not likenesses of sensible things nor duplicates of known beings;

to give form and shape to laws, or deduce from the laws themselves their form and shape: is this not equally characteristic of both arts?

Phaedrus

They can also be compared in this respect.

Socrates

We have tracked down the mystery with these few ideas. The analogy we were hunting for is perhaps connected with those half-concrete, half-abstract existences, which play so large a part in our two arts: they are singular existences, true creatures of man, partaking of sight and of touch—or else of hearing—but also of reason, number, and language.

Phaedrus

You mean geometric figures?

Socrates

Yes. And groups of sounds, or rhythms and musical modes. Sound itself, pure sound, is a sort of creation. Nature has only noises.

Phaedrus

But are not all figures geometrical?

Socrates

No more than a noise is a musical sound.

Phaedrus

But how do you distinguish the one from the other, figures that are geometric from those that are not?

Socrates

Let us first consider the latter. . . . Let us suppose ourselves still alive, dear Phaedrus, provided with bodies and surrounded by bodies. Take a stylus, I would then say, or a pointed stone, and draw upon some wall any line at all without thinking. Draw with a single gesture. Are you doing it?

Phaedrus

I am, immaterial though I be, by using my memory.

Socrates

What have you done?

Phaedrus

It seems to me that I have traced a line of smoke. It advances, breaks, comes back, knots, twines, and twists; gets mixed up with itself, giving me the image of an aimless whim, without beginning or end, and without any meaning other than the liberty of my gesture within the radius of my arm. . . .

Socrates

Just so. Your hand did not itself know, when it was at such and such a place, where it would go next. It was confusedly impelled by the mere tendency to leave the position it occupied. It was, furthermore, retarded and held back and slowed down as it were by its growing distance from the body. . . . And finally, the stone itself, scratching the stone surface with a facility that varied according to the direction, added this element of chance to those that were due to yourself. . . . Can such a thing be a geometrical figure, Phaedrus?

Phaedrus

Most certainly not. But I do not know why.

Socrates

And if I now asked you to draw with this stone or instrument the outline of some object—of a vase, for instance, or the blunt profile of Socrates—would the line that you drew be more geometrical than the line scratched at random on the wall?

Phaedrus

No—not in itself.

Socrates

You reply as I should myself have done: "Not in itself." You feel then that there is something more in the act you fulfill when held to a model, than in the foregoing act, which had no aim but that of scratching the surface of a wall. And yet the figure drawn—the outline of a vase, or the quaintly sinuous outline of the nose of Socrates—is not in itself more geometrical than the line blindly drawn in the first case. Every instant of your movement is foreign to the other instants. Nothing inevitable links the concavity of my nose with the convexity of my forehead. And yet your hand is no longer free to stray about on the wall; now "you will" something and impose upon your drawing this law from without: that it must reproduce a given form. You oblige yourself to this, and you have even defined that law you have imposed on yourself by these few words: "Represent the shadow of the head of Socrates upon a plane surface." This law is not sufficient to guide your hand, since the presence of the model is also necessary; but it governs the totality of that hand's action; it makes that action a whole with its own end, its sanction, and its limits.

Phaedrus

Could I not truly say, therefore, that I am performing a

geometric act, but that the figure which results is not geometrical?

Socrates

Certainly. Or you can say that it is so, in so far as it is a likeness, and that it is not so in itself.

Phaedrus

Come now to the truly geometric figures.

Socrates

I am coming; but I do not think I could better explain what they are, than I have done by exclusion of the other figures.

Phaedrus

You must explain all the same.

Socrates

I call "geometric" those figures which are records of the movements we can express in few words.

Phaedrus

So, if you order someone to walk, that single word engenders geometric figures?

Socrates

No. If I say: "Walk!" the movement is not well enough defined by the order. The man may go forward, backward, sideways, or aslant. . . . What is necessary is that, by a single proposition, the movement should be defined so precisely that there remains no other liberty to the body in motion but to follow it, and it alone. And this proposition must be obeyed by each instant of this movement, so that all the parts of the figure may be one identical thing in thought, though different in extension. If then I tell you to walk remaining always at an equal distance from two trees, you will engender one of those figures, provided that in your movement you observe the condition that I have set you.

Phaedrus

Well, and what then? What is marvelous about this engendering?

Socrates

I know nothing more divine, nothing more human: nothing more simple, yet nothing mightier.

Phaedrus

I am curious to know your reasons.

Socrates

O my friend, do you not find it admirable that sight and movement should be so closely united that I can change into movement a visible object, like a line; and a movement into an object? That this transformation should be certain, and ever the same, and that it should be so by the means of speech? Sight gives me a movement, and the movement makes me feel its own generation and the connections of the figure it traces. I am made to move by sight; I am enriched with an image by movement, and the same thing is given me, whether I come at it through time or find it in space. . . .

Phaedrus

But in what way are words necessary? And why the few words?

Socrates

This, dear Phaedrus, is the most important point: no geometry without the word. Without it, figures are accidents, and neither make manifest nor serve the power of the mind. By it, the movements which beget figures are reduced to acts, and these acts being clearly designated by words, each figure is a proposition that can be combined with others; and we are able in this way, without paying any more heed to sight or movement, to recognize the properties of the combinations we have made; and as it were, to construct or enrich space, by means of well-linked sentences.

Phaedrus

Then the geometer, when he has sufficiently considered the figure, closes his eyes, in some sort, and makes himself blind?

Socrates

For a time he gets away from images, and yields blindly to the destiny imposed on words by the machinery of the mind. In the very heart of a laborious silence, the more complex words resolve themselves into the most simple; ideas which were identical, but distinct, become confounded; similar intellectual forms summarize and simplify one another; common notions involved in different propositions serve as links between these, and disappear, thus allowing us to join together the other things with which those notions were separately connected. . . . Nothing more remains of thought but its pure acts, by which, in its own presence, it changes and transforms itself into itself. It finally comes to draw from out its own dark recesses the entire mechanism of its operations. . . .

105

Phaedrus

This admirable blind man contemplates himself as the theater of a learned choreography of symbols! . . . Do you recall the distraught eyes of Diocles?

Socrates

Yet these marvels are but the supreme effects of language.

Phaedrus

And so language is a constructor? . . . I already knew that it was the source of fables; and for some, even the father of the . . .

Socrates

Phaedrus, Phaedrus, impiety lacks grace in these abodes. Since there are here no thunderbolts, there is no merit in blaspheming. . . . And these dim meadows grow no hemlock. But most certainly the word can build, just as it can create, as it can corrupt. . . . An altar raised to the word should present three fronts diversely adorned; and if I had to figure forth the word in human semblance, I should give it three faces: the one, almost shapeless, would signify the common word—that which is no sooner born than it dies, and is there and then swallowed up by its very use. Immediately it is transformed into the bread that we ask for, the road we are shown, the anger of him who suffers an insult. . . . But the second face would fling from its rounded mouth a crystalline flood of eternal water: it would have the noblest features, a grand and impassioned eye; a neck powerful and massive, such as statuaries give to the Muses.

Phaedrus

And the third?

Socrates

By Apollo, how am I to figure it? . . . It would have to be some inhuman countenance, with features severe and subtle as those which the Egyptians, it is said, were able to give to the faces of their gods.

Phaedrus

And truly said. Craft, deep enigmas, an almost cruel precision, an implacable and half-bestial cunning, all the signs of feline watchfulness and of a fierce spirituality are visible in the images of those stern deities. The skillfully proportioned blend of acuteness and coldness produces in the soul a peculiar sense of uneasiness and disquietude. And these monsters of silence and lucidity, infinitely calm, infinitely alert, rigid and seemingly endowed with imminence, or with a suppleness about to be, have the semblance of Intelligence herself, in guise of beast and animal—impenetrable—all-penetrating.

Socrates

What is there more mysterious than clarity? . . . What more capricious than the way in which light and shade are distributed over hours and over men? Certain peoples lose themselves in their thoughts; but for us Greeks all things are forms. We retain only their relations; and enclosed as it were in the limpid day, Orpheuslike we build, by means of the word, temples of wisdom and science that may suffice for all reasonable creatures. This great art requires of us an admirably exact language. The very word that signifies language is also the name, with us, for reason and calculation; a single word says these three things. For what is reason if not discourse itself, when the meanings of the terms are properly limited and assured of their permanence, and when

107

these immutable meanings are fitted to one another, and
combined clearly? And that is one and the same thing as
calculation.

Phaedrus

How so?

Socrates

Because amongst words are the numbers, which are the
simplest words.

Phaedrus

But cannot the other words, which are not simple, be
used for calculation?

Socrates

With difficulty.

Phaedrus

Why?

Socrates

Because they were created separately; some at such and
such a time, to fulfill such and such a need; the others under
other circumstances. A single view of things, a single desire, a
single mind, did not institute them as by a single act. Taken
together, they are therefore not suited to any special use, and
it is impossible to conduct them through sure and far-reach-
ing developments without getting lost in their endless rami-
fications. . . . So it is necessary to fit these complex words
together like irregular blocks, speculating on the chances
and surprises that arrangements of this kind hold in store for
us, and to give the name of "poets" to those whom fortune
favors in this work.

Phaedrus

You seem to have been won over yourself to the adoration of architecture! Here you are, unable to speak without borrowing from the major art its images and its firm ideal.

Socrates

I am still steeped in the sayings of Eupalinos that you were recalling. They have aroused within me something that is akin to them.

Phaedrus

So there was an architect in you?

Socrates

Nothing can beguile, nothing attract us, nothing makes us prick up our ears, or holds our gaze, nothing by us is chosen from among the multitude of things, and causes a stir in our souls, that was not in some sort pre-existent in our being or secretly awaited by our nature. All that we become, even fleetingly, was prepared beforehand. There was within me an architect whom circumstances did not fashion forth.

Phaedrus

How do you know this?

Socrates

By I know not what deep intent to build, which darkly troubles my thoughts.

Phaedrus

You showed no sign of it when we existed.

Socrates

I told you that I was born *several* and that I died *one*. The child when it appears is a countless crowd, which life reduces soon enough to a single individual, the one who manifests himself and who dies. A multitude of Socrateses were born with me, from whom little by little the Socrates stood out who was destined for the magistrates and the hemlock.

Phaedrus

And what has become of the others?

Socrates

Ideas. They have remained in the condition of ideas. They came, asking to be, and they were refused. I kept them within myself, as my doubts and contradictions. . . . Sometimes these germs of persons are favored by circumstance, and then we are on the verge of changing our natures. We find in ourselves tastes and gifts which we did not suspect: the musician becomes a general, the pilot feels himself to be a physician; and he whose virtue was wont to admire and respect itself discovers within himself a hidden Cacus, and the soul of a thief.

Phaedrus

It is very true that certain periods in man's life are like the crossing of ways.

Socrates

Adolescence is more particularly placed in the midst of divergent roads. . . . One day, one of my glorious days, dear Phaedrus, I experienced a strange hesitation between my souls. Chance placed in my hands the most ambiguous object imaginable. And the infinite reflections that it caused me to make were equally capable of leading me to that philosopher that I became, and to the artist that I have never been. . . .

Phaedrus

It was an object that solicited you so variously?

Socrates

Yes. A paltry object, just something I found as I was walking. It was the origin of a thought divided, of itself, between constructing and knowing.

Phaedrus

Marvelous object! Object comparable to that box of Pandora, in which all good things and all evils were enclosed together! . . . Make me see this object, as the great Homer makes us admire the shield of the son of Peleus!

Socrates

It is impossible to describe. . . . Its importance is inseparable from the embarrassment which it caused me.

Phaedrus

Explain yourself more abundantly.

Socrates

Well then, Phaedrus, this is how it was. I was walking on the very edge of the sea. I was following an endless shore. . . . This is not a dream I am telling you. I was going I know not whither, overflowing with life, half-intoxicated by my youth. The air, deliciously rude and pure, pressing against my face and limbs, confronted me—an impalpable hero that I must vanquish in order to advance. And this resistance, ever overcome, made of me, too, at every step an imaginary hero, victorious over the wind, and rich in energies that were ever reborn, ever equal to the power of the invisible adversary. . . .

111

That is just what youth is. I trod firmly the winding beach, beaten and hardened by the waves. All things around me were simple and pure: the sky, the sand, the water. I watched, as they came from the offing, those mighty shapes which seem to be running from the coasts of Libya, charioting their glistening summits, their hollow valleys, their relentless energy from Africa all the way to Attica across the immense liquid expanse. At last they come upon their obstacle, the very plinth of Hellas; they shatter themselves against those submarine foundations; they recoil in disorder towards the origin of their motion. When the waves are thus destroyed and confounded, yet seized in turn by those that follow them, it is as though the forms of the deep were engaged in strife. The countless drops break their chains, a sparkling spray goes up. One sees white horsemen leaping beyond themselves, and all those envoys of the inexhaustible sea perishing and reappearing, with a monotonous tumult, on a gentle, almost imperceptible slope, which all their vehemence, though it be come from the most remote horizon, will yet never be able to surmount. . . . Here the foam, flung farthest by the highest wave, forms yellowish iridescent heaps which burst in the sunlight, or which the wind sweeps along and disperses in the drollest fashion, like beasts scared by the sudden bound of the sea. But as for me, I was reveling in the newborn virgin foam. . . . Its contact is of a strange softness. It is a milk—warm, airy—that comes in with a voluptuous violence, pours round one's bare feet, bathes them, passes beyond, and flows down upon them again, moaning with a voice that forsakes the shore and withdraws into itself; while the human statue, a living presence, sinks a little deeper into the sand that draws it down; and whilst the soul gives itself up to that so puissant and so delicate music, is soothed by it, and follows it eternally.

Phaedrus

You make me live again. O language charged with salt! O words truly born of the sea!

Socrates

I have let my talk run on. . . . We have all eternity during which to discourse upon time. We are here—Danaïdlike— to empty out our spirits.

Phaedrus

But the object?

Socrates

The object lay upon the beach where I was walking, where I have halted, where I have spoken to you at length of a sight with which you are as familiar as I, but which, when recalled in this place, acquires a kind of novelty from the fact that it has forever disappeared. So wait, and in a few words I shall have found this thing that I was not looking for.

Phaedrus

We are still on the seashore?

Socrates

Necessarily. This frontier between Neptune and Earth, ever disputed by those rival divinities, is the scene of the most dismal and most incessant commerce. That which the sea rejects, that which the land cannot retain, the enigmatic bits of drift; the hideous limbs of dislocated ships, black as charcoal, and looking as though charred by the salt waters; carrion horribly pecked and washed sleek by the waves; elastic weeds torn by the tempests from the transparent pasture grounds of Proteus' flocks; collapsed monsters, of cold, deathly hues; all the things, in short, that fortune delivers over to the fury of the shore, and to the fruitless litigation between wave and beach, are there carried to and fro; raised, lowered; seized, lost, seized again according to the hour and the day; sad witnesses to the indifference of the fates, ignoble treasures, playthings of an interchange as perpetual as it is stationary. . . .

Phaedrus

And it was there that you made your find?

Socrates

Yes, there. I found one of those things cast up by the sea; a white thing of the most pure whiteness; polished and hard and smooth and light. It shone in the sun on the licked sand, that is somber and spark-bestrewn. I took it up; I blew upon it; I rubbed it against my cloak, and its singular shape suspended all my other thoughts. Who made thee? I pondered. Thou resemblest nothing, and yet thou art not shapeless. Art thou a sport of nature, O nameless thing, that art come to me by the will of the gods, in the midst of the refuse that the sea this night has flung from her?

Phaedrus

How large was this object?

Socrates

About as big as my fist.

Phaedrus

And made of what matter?

Socrates

Of the same matter as its form: matter for doubt. It was perhaps some fishbone weirdly worn by the rubbing of the fine sand under the water? Or a piece of ivory carved for I know not what purpose, by some craftsman beyond the seas? Who knows? . . . A divinity, perhaps, that perished with the very vessel which it had been made to preserve from shipwreck? But who can have been the maker of this? Was it a mortal obedient to an idea, who, pursuing with his own hands an aim foreign to the substance he is attacking, scratches, cuts off, or joins together again; pauses and considers; and finally takes leave of his work—something telling him that the work is finished? . . . Or was it not rather the product of a living body, which, unwittingly, labors with its own substance, and blindly forms for itself its organs and its armor, its shell, its bones, its weapons; causing its nourishment, which it gathers from around it, to participate in the mysterious construction which ensures it a certain lastingness?

But perhaps it was but the fruit of an infinite lapse of time. . . . Through the eternal laboring of the sea waves, a fragment of rock, by dint of being rolled and knocked to and fro, if its substance is of an unequal hardness and so is not liable in time to become rounded, may very well take on some striking semblance. It is not altogether impossible that, if a quite shapeless piece of marble or stone be given up to the permanent commotion of the waters, it should some day be thence recovered, by a chance of another kind, and should then bear the likeness of Apollo. I mean that the fisherman who had some notion of those divine features, might recognize them in this piece of marble drawn from the waters; but as for the thing itself, the sacred face is for it one fleeting form out of the family of forms that the action of the seas must impose upon it. Centuries cost nothing, and he who disposes of them changes what he will into what he will.

115

Phaedrus

But then, dear Socrates, when an artist makes immediately, and by a consistent application of his will, such a bust (as that of Apollo), is not his work in some sort the contrary of indefinite time?

Socrates

Precisely. It is the exact contrary, as though acts illuminated by a thought abridged the course of nature; and so we may safely say that an artist is worth a thousand centuries, or a hundred thousand, or even many more! —In other words, that this almost inconceivable stretch of time would have been necessary for ignorance or chance blindly to bring to pass the selfsame thing that our skilled man has accomplished in a few days. Here is a strange standard for measuring works!

Phaedrus

Strange indeed. It is a great misfortune that we can hardly make use of it. . . . But tell me, what did you do with that thing in your hand?

Socrates

I stood still for some little time, examining it on all sides. I questioned it without stopping at an answer. . . . I could not determine whether this singular object were the work of life, or of art, or rather of time—and so a freak of nature. . . . Then suddenly I flung it back into the sea.

Phaedrus

The water splashed up, and you had a feeling of relief.

Socrates

The mind does not reject a riddle so easily. The soul does

not recover its calm again as simply as the sea. . . . This question that had just been born, finding in my spirit no lack either of sustenance or of resonance, of leisure or of space, began to grow, and busied me for hours. In vain I breathed in the delicious air and feasted my gaze on the resplendent beauties of the expanse; I felt myself still the prisoner of a thought. My memories nourished it with examples, which it endeavored to turn to its own advantage. I offered it a thousand things, for I was not yet, at that time, so expert in the art of reflecting, and of luring myself on, as to discern what one should and what one should not demand of a truth still too young, too delicate to withstand the full rigor of a lengthy cross-examination.

Phaedrus

Let us have a view of this frail truth of yours.

Socrates

I hardly venture to proffer, even for your amusement . . .

Phaedrus

But you yourself suggested it!

Socrates

Yes. I thought it would bear exposition better. . . . But as I come closer to it and am almost on the point of telling it, diffidence overcomes me, and I feel some shame in acquainting you with this naïve product of my golden age.

Phaedrus

What vanity! You forget that we are shades. . . .

Socrates

Well, this was my ingenuous idea. Intrigued by this object the nature of which I could not get to know, and which was equally claimed and rejected by all the categories, I sought to escape from the perplexing image of my find. How was this to be managed, unless by proceeding indirectly and magnifying the difficulty itself? After all, I said to myself, the same embarrassment which this object I have found causes me can be conceived about an object that is known. But with this latter, since it is known, we are in possession of both the question and the answer; or rather we are more particularly in possession of the answer, and, feeling that we have it, we omit to ask the question. . . . Suppose now that I am looking at some very familiar thing such as a house, a table, a wine jar; and that I pretend for a brief space that I am a complete savage who has never seen such objects, I might well doubt whether those objects were of human fabrication. . . . Not knowing to what use they can be put, nor even if they are of use to anyone, and being moreover informed by nobody, I should needs have to imagine some means for setting my mind at rest concerning them. . . .

Phaedrus

And what did you imagine?

Socrates

Seeking, finding, losing, and rediscovering the means of discriminating between what is produced by nature and what is made by men, I remained standing for some time in the same place, my eye hesitating amid various lights; then I started walking very rapidly inland, like someone whose thoughts, after having long been tossed in all directions, seem at last to have found their bearings; and to resolve themselves into a single idea, engendering at the same instant in his body a decision of clearly determined movement and a resolute bearing. . . .

Phaedrus

I know that feeling. I have always marveled how an idea which comes to one, however abstract it may be, gives one wings, and bears one any- and everywhere. One stops, and then one is off again; that is what thinking is!

Socrates

Well, half running I reasoned thus: a tree, with its leaves, is a product of nature. It is an edifice of which the parts are the leaves, the branches, the trunk, and the roots. I assume that each of its parts gives me the idea of a certain complexity. I then say that the whole of this tree is more complex than any one of its parts.

Phaedrus

That is evident.

Socrates

I am very far from thinking so now. But then I was scarce eighteen, and all my knowledge was certitudes! —The tree then, which comprises such and such parts, comprises and includes all their various complexities; and it is the same with an animal, whose whole body is a more complex thing than the foot, or the head, since the complexity of the whole comprises in some sort, as parts of itself, the complexities of its divers parts.

Phaedrus

The fact being, my dear Socrates, that we can scarce conceive a tree as part of a leaf, or the accessory of a root; nor a horse as organ or part of its thigh. . . .

119

Socrates

I forthwith inferred that, in all these beings, the degree or level of the whole is necessarily to be ranged higher than the level of the details; or rather that it can be equal to or higher than the latter, but never inferior to it.

Phaedrus

Your thought seems to me clear enough; but it is difficult to conceive this degree of complication precisely.

Socrates

I have told you more than once that I was eighteen! I was thinking, as best I could, of degree in the order and distribution of the parts and in the elements brought together to form a being. . . . But all these beings of which I have spoken are of the class that nature produces. They increase in such wise that the matter they are made of, the forms they put on, the functions they are to fulfill, the means they possess for adapting themselves to places and seasons, are invisibly bound up with one another by secret relations; and that is perhaps the meaning of the words, "produced by nature."

But with the objects which are the work of man it is quite different. Their structure is . . . a disorder!

Phaedrus

How can that be?

Socrates

When you think, do you not feel that you are secretly disarranging something; and when you fall asleep, do you not feel that you are leaving that something to arrange itself as best it can?

Phaedrus

I cannot tell. . . .

Socrates

No matter! I continue. The acts of the man who builds or fashions something are not concerned with "all" the qualities of the substance that those acts modify, but only with some. That which is sufficient for our purpose is what matters to us. It is the effects of language that suffice the orator; its relations and its sequence that suffice the logician; and just as the one neglects rigor, the other neglects ornament. And likewise, in the material order: a wheel, a door, a tub require each a certain solidity, a certain weight, a certain adaptability in their adjustment and use; and if chestnut, elm, and oak are equally or almost equally suitable for this, the wheelwright or carpenter will use them more or less indifferently with an eye only to the expense. But in nature you do not see the lemon tree bearing apples, although in a given year they would perhaps cost her less than lemons to produce.

Man, I assert, fabricates by abstraction, ignoring and forgetting a great part of the qualities of what he uses, and concerning himself solely with clear and definite conditions, which can most often be simultaneously satisfied, not by a single material, but by several kinds. He drinks milk or wine or water or ale indifferently out of gold, glass, horn, or onyx; and whether the vase be wide or slender, or shaped like a leaf or a flower, or with a quaintly twisted foot, the drinker considers the drinking alone. Even he who made that cup was unable to do more than harmonize very roughly its substance, its form, and its function. For the intimate subordination of these three things and their profound interfusion could be but the work of Creative Nature herself. The artisan cannot do his work without violating or disarranging an order by the forces which he applies to matter in order to adapt it to the idea he wishes to imitate, and to the usage he intends. He is therefore inevitably led to produce objects of which the whole is always a degree below the level of their parts. If he make a table, the assembling of its parts results in a much less complex arrangement than that of the texture of the fibers of the wood, and it brings crudely together in a certain unnatural order, pieces of a big tree, which had grown and developed when otherwise related.

Phaedrus

A strange example of this disorder occurs to me.

Socrates

What example?

Phaedrus

The very order, that so admirable order, which the art of the general imposes on individuals themselves, when they are being trained to serve in the ranks. Do you remember, dear Socrates, those days spent at drill and formations in close or extended order, exercises which accustom the young to military obedience and to unanimity in action?

Socrates

By Hercules! I was a soldier, and a good soldier.

Phaedrus

Well, those long bristling lines, those phalanxes of formidable girth, those armored rectangles, which we formed on the dusty plains, were they not very simple figures, whereas each element of those figures was the most complex object in the world, a man? And furthermore, among them were men like Socrates, Phidias, Pericles, and Zeno, admirable elements in whom to the ordinary complexity of humans is joined all the complexity of the possible universes that they have in their minds!

Socrates

Not a bad example. I remember having on several occasions to appeal to my reason, in order to induce my rich and multiple soul to accept this role of simple unit and indistinguishable part of an army. So you see that the idea of order and disorder, when properly handled, explains or at least reconciles many things.

Phaedrus

I see that, impelled by that object found on the seashore, to which none but you would have paid the least attention, your adolescent genius rose almost at once to the consideration of a very important and very simple distinction. From the slightest of incidents you extracted this thought: that human creations resolve themselves into a conflict between two kinds of order, one of which, being natural and given, suffers and sustains the other, which is the expression of the needs and desires of man.

Socrates

That is what I believed. Man does not need the whole of nature, but only a part. The philosopher is one who conceives a wider view, and wishes to have need of everything. But the man who only wishes to live has need neither of iron nor of bronze "in themselves"; but merely of such and such a hardness or ductility. He is forced to take them where they are to be found, that is to say in a metal which has also other qualities indifferent to him. . . . He considers his aim alone. If he wishes to drive in a nail, he strikes it with a stone, or with a hammer made of iron, or of bronze, or even of very hard wood; and he drives it in with little blows, or with a single more forcible one, or sometimes by a pressure; what does it matter to him? The result is the same, the nail is driven home. But if one is not concerned to follow the thread of this action, and if one simply views all the circumstances, these operations appear to be each entirely different—phenomena that cannot be compared with one another.

Phaedrus

I now understand how you could hesitate between constructing and knowing.

Socrates

One has to choose between being a man and being a mind. Man can act only because he can ignore, and content himself with a part of this knowledge which is his peculiar extravagance, a knowledge that is somewhat more extensive than is necessary!

Phaedrus

Yet it is this slight excess that makes us men!

Socrates

Men? . . . Think you that dogs do not see the stars, for which they have no use? It would be enough for them that their eye should perceive terrestrial things; but it is not so exactly adapted to pure utility as to be blind to the celestial bodies and the majestic ordering of night.

Phaedrus

They never tire of howling at the moon!

Socrates

And do not humans strive in a thousand ways to fill or to break the eternal silence of those infinite spaces that affright them?

Phaedrus

Your own life was spent so! . . . But for my part, I cannot console myself for the death of that architect who was in you, and whom you assassinated by meditating overmuch on the fragment of a shell! With your profundity and prodigious subtleties, Socrates, you would have far surpassed our most famous builders. Neither Ictinos, nor Eupalinos of Megara, nor Chersiphron of Gnossos, nor Spintharos of Corinth would have been able to rival Socrates the Athenian.

Socrates

Phaedrus, I beg of you! . . . This subtle matter of which we are now made does not permit of our laughing. I feel I ought to laugh, but I cannot. . . . So refrain!

Phaedrus

But, quite seriously, Socrates, what would you have done, as an architect?

Socrates

How can I tell? . . . I only see in a general way how I should have conducted my thoughts.

Phaedrus

Conduct them at least to the threshold of the edifice that you did not build.

Socrates

I have merely to pursue that sort of reverie of reasoning that I have but now been engaged in.

We have said—or as good as said—that all visible things proceed from three modes of generation or production, which moreover mingle and interpenetrate. . . . The one kind chiefly make chance manifest, as can be seen from the fragments of a rock, or from some landscape, not specially chosen, peopled with plants that have sprung up at random. The other kind—like the plant itself, or the animal, or the piece of salt, whose purple-tinted facets cohere mysteriously—lead us to imagine a growth that is simultaneous, sure, and blind, and encompassed within a duration that seems potentially to contain them. It is as though what they will be is waiting on what they were; and, further, as though they increase in harmony with their surroundings. . . . And finally there are the works of man, which, in some sort, cut across this nature and this chance, utilizing them, but doing them violence, and at the same time violated by them in accordance with what we said a moment ago.

Now the tree does not construct its branches and leaves; nor the cock his beak and his feathers. But the tree and all its parts, and the cock and all his, are constructed by the principles themselves, which do not exist apart from the constructing. That which makes and that which is made are indivisible; and it is so with all bodies that live, or that have a sort of life, like crystals. It is not acts that engender them; and their generation cannot be explained by any combination of acts, for acts presuppose living beings.

Nor yet can it be said that they are spontaneous—this word is simply an avowal of impotence. . . .

We know, moreover, that these beings have need of a thousand things in their environment, in order that they should be. They are dependent upon everything, though the action of all things seems, by itself, incapable of creating them.

But as for the objects made by man, they are due to the acts of a thought.

The principles are separate from the construction, and are as it were imposed by a tyrant from without upon the material, to which he imparts them by acts. Nature in her work does not distinguish the details from the whole; but pushes from all sides at once, chaining herself to herself, without experiments, without regressions, with no models, no special aim, and no reserves; she does not separate a project from its execution; she never takes a direct course regardless of obstacles, but compromises with them, mixes them with her motion, goes round them or makes use of them; as though the path she takes, the object that follows this path, the time spent in covering it, the very difficulties it presents, were all of the same substance. If a man waves his arm, we distinguish this arm from his gesture, and we conceive between gesture and arm a *purely possible* relation. But from the point of view of nature, this gesture of the arm and the arm itself cannot be separated. . . .

Phaedrus

So, to construct would be to create by separate principles?

Socrates

Yes, the peculiarity of man is to create in two kinds of time, one of which runs on in the domain of pure possibility, in the very heart of that subtle substance which can imitate all things and combine them with one another to infinity. The other time is nature's. It in one sense contains the first, and in another sense, is contained in it. Our acts partake of both. The project is separate from the act, and the act from the result.

Phaedrus

But how can we conceive the separateness, and how find the principles?

Socrates

They are not always so distinct as I have said. All men, moreover, do not distinguish them equally. But a very simple and very primitive reflection will suffice to give an idea of it. Man discerns three great things in the All: he finds there his body, he finds there his soul—and then there is the rest of the world. Between these things there is an unceasing commerce, and sometimes even a confusion arises; but always after a certain time has elapsed, these three things come to be clearly distinguished from one another. It is as though their intermixture cannot last, and that this division must necessarily manifest itself from time to time.

Phaedrus

A man who is asleep sometimes takes his leg for a stone, and his state of rest for a movement. He takes his desire for a light; the noise of his blood for a mysterious voice; the feeling of his own face being brushed by a fly becomes the vision of a terrifying face which pursues him. . . . But all that cannot last. He wakes up, flinging the past far from his body, reserving it for his soul; anew he divides all things and rebuilds himself according to his principles.

Socrates

It is therefore reasonable to think that the creations of man are made either with a view to his body, and that is the principle we call *utility*, or with a view to his soul, and that is what he seeks under the name of *beauty*. But, further, since he who constructs or creates has to deal with the rest of the world and with the movement of nature, which both tend perpetually to dissolve, corrupt, or upset what he makes, he must recognize and seek to communicate to his works a third principle, that expresses the resistance he wishes them to offer to their destiny, which is, to perish. So he seeks *solidity* or *lastingness*.

Phaedrus

Yes, those are indeed the main characteristics of a complete work.

Socrates

Architecture alone demands them, and carries them to their highest point.

Phaedrus

I look upon it as the most complete of the arts.

Socrates

Thus the body constrains us to desire what is useful, or simply convenient; and the soul demands of us the beautiful; but the rest of the world, with its laws and its hazards, obliges us to consider in every work the question of its solidity.

Phaedrus

But are not these principles, so distinct in your expression of them, always mixed in fact? It sometimes used to seem to me that an impression of beauty was born of exactitude; and that a sort of delight was engendered by the almost miraculous conformity of an object with the function that it must fulfill. And so the perfection of this aptitude excites in our souls the feeling of a relationship between the beautiful and the necessary; and the final ease or simplicity of the result, compared with the intricacy of the problem, fills us with an indescribable enthusiasm. Unexpected elegance intoxicates us. Nothing but what is of strict utility finds a place in such happy fabrications: they no longer contain anything not solely deduced from the exigencies of the desired effect; but one feels that almost a god was needed to make so pure a deduction. There exist admirable tools, strangely definite, and clean-cut as bones; and waiting like them for acts and forces, and for nothing more.

Socrates

They have, in some sort, made themselves; agelong use has necessarily discovered the best form. Multiple practice attains the ideal some day, and stops there. The thousands of attempts of thousands of men converge slowly towards the most economical and surest form: once this has been attained, everyone imitates it; and the millions of these replicas are the final answer to the myriads of previous gropings, which they cancel. This can be seen even in the poets' capricious art, and not only in the tool bag of the wheelwright and the goldsmith. . . . Nay, who knows, Phaedrus, if the effort of humans in their search for God, the observances, the prayers they essay, their obstinate will to discover the most efficacious . . . who knows if mortals will not finally discover a certitude—or an incertitude—stable and in exact conformity with their nature, if not with the very nature of God?

Phaedrus

There are also discourses so brief, and some of but a single word, yet so full and answering to everything in their concise energy so profoundly, that they seem to concentrate years of internal discussions and secret eliminations; they are indivisible and decisive, like sovran acts. Men will live long on those few words! . . . And the geometers? Do you not believe that there may be found in them a singular pursuit and marvelous examples of that rigorous kind of beauty?

Socrates

Why, that is the most precious thing they have! —They approach each particular aim they pursue by bringing together the most general truths; these they seem at first to be gathering and adjusting with no underlying thought. They dissimulate their design, they hide their real end. We do not see at first what they are driving at. . . . Why draw this line? Why remind us of that proposition? . . . Why do this, and not that? —Nothing more is said of the problem at issue. You would think they had forgotten it, and were losing themselves in dialectical remoteness. . . . But suddenly they make a simple remark. The bird falls from the clouds, the prey is at their feet; and while we are still asking ourselves what they are trying to do, they are already looking at us with a smile!

Phaedrus

A smile of contempt.

Socrates

Such artists have no reason to be modest. They have found the means of inextricably mixing up necessity and artifice. They invent tricks and spells, which are like the jugglery of reason. The greatest liberty is born of the greatest rigor. But as for their secret, it is well enough known. They substitute for nature, against which the other artists strive,

131

a nature more or less drawn from the first nature, but all of whose forms and beings are ultimately but acts of the mind, these acts being clearly determined and preserved by their names. In this essential fashion they construct worlds perfect in themselves, which sometimes are so far removed from ours as to be inconceivable, and sometimes come so close to it as to coincide in part with the real.

Phaedrus

And it sometimes happens that the extremes of speculation put weapons into the hands of practice. . . .

Socrates

This extension of their powers is the triumph of that mode of construction of which I spoke to you.

Phaedrus

By separate principles?

Socrates

By separate principles.

Phaedrus

I can well recognize these principles and this separateness in speculative things; but does the real lend itself equally well to these distinctions?

Socrates

Not so easily. Everything that is sensible exists as it were in several ways. Everything that is real is bound to an infinity of sequences, fulfills a thousand functions; it carries with it many more characteristics and consequences than an act of thought can embrace. But in certain cases, and for a certain time, man subjugates this manifold reality and triumphs over it to some extent.

Phaedrus

I once heard the same things at the Piraeus. Out of a briny mouth came words that differed little from yours. It said bluntly that one had to be crafty with nature, and according to circumstance imitate her in order to constrain her, oppose her to herself, and rob her of secrets that could be used to combat her mystery.

Socrates

Did you then know more than one Eupalinos?

Phaedrus

I am naturally inquisitive about craftsmen. I eagerly seek out persons whose ideas and actions question and answer one another precisely. My sage of the Piraeus was a Phoenician of a strange versatility. He began as a slave in Sicily. From a slave, he mysteriously rose to be the skipper of a vessel; and from master seaman he turned calker. Tired of graving, and leaving old hulls for new, he set up as a shipbuilder. His wife kept a tavern a few steps off from his yard. I have seen no mortal more various in his means, more knowing in artifices: more inquisitive about all that did not concern him, more cunning in making it serve for the things that did concern him. . . . He viewed all affairs solely in the light of practice and processes. Even vice and virtue were for him occupations which have their special seasons and graces, and which are practiced as circumstances demand. "Sometimes," he would say, "one runs free, and sometimes one is close-hauled. The main thing is to sail tidily!"

I imagine that he must have saved some lives in the

chances and changes of a sea life, and taken some others, owing to those difficulties that arise in bordellos, or in awkward negotiations between pirates. But all of it well executed!

Socrates

His shade, I fear, must be near neighbor to Ixion's!

Phaedrus

Pshaw! He'll have got through all right! . . . He never lost his head. He was always saying to himself: "Steady, now! Steady!" . . . What a game fellow he was! . . . Never a regret, never a reproach, never a remorse, never a wish. . . . But all action, and money down!

Socrates

And what brings this rascal into our analysis?

Phaedrus

You'll see in a moment what a helping hand the good man is going to give us! Know then, delectable Socrates, that he was provided with the profoundest and most delicate ears ever owned by skull of man. All that penetrated into those bushy labyrinths fell a prey to a monster of portentous greed. The beast that lurked in that sturdy shell grew fat on all manner of precise things. I know not how many languages, how many recipes, it had digested! What a variety of wisdoms it had transmuted into one choice substance! It had sucked the contents of so many other brains! I used to imagine it surrounded with the debris and empty shells of a thousand minds that it had drained!

Socrates

You are painting me an octopus!

Phaedrus

But an octopus that questions the populous waters, that chooses and darts, brandishing its whips in the dense deep, and taking vertiginous possession of whatever suits its purpose—is not such a creature a hundred times more alive than the sponge that never budges? How many sponges have we not known, stuck fast forever beneath a portico of Athens, absorbing and exuding without effort all the opinions that fluctuated around them; sponges bathed in words, indifferently imbued with Socrates, Anaxagoras, Melittos, with whoever spoke last! . . . Sponges and fools have this in common, O Socrates, that they cling!

But as for my son of the sea, most inquisitive child of that roaring harlot who calls to men eternally, he had appropriated and assimilated what was best for himself. After coming through astounding adventures and truly miraculous fishing exploits; bleached, blackened, gilded in turn by successive climes; after observing with his own eyes meteors such as are almost never seen; after trying his cunning upon the most subtle fishes; winning over the most hardheaded tradesmen, tricking the most deceitful; and haggling here and there about wages—to be given, or . . . received—with many a sour prostitute—this man (will you believe it?) when he returned from his perils, pulling himself together after the lowest debaucheries, would go and converse with the men of learning, the sages and the scholars whom he had learnt to revere?

Socrates

And where had he learnt that?

Phaedrus

On the sea. There, when you are lost far from land—the ship like a blind man abandoned on the roof of a house—a

135

piece of advice given by one of those sages may chance to be for you the signal of salvation. A saying of Pythagoras, a precept and a number remembered from Thales, if some planet suddenly shows, and if your self-possession has not left you, may well lead you back to life.

Socrates

But you, where is it you are leading me?

Phaedrus

I wanted to conduct you to the wooden structures that the Phoenician used to build. But first I had to describe the man. . . . If you had but seen him just once, with his red-rimmed eyes, which were like the copper-colored depths of the glowing sea wherein is found the green fish that is dangerous to eat! . . . But we were speaking, dear Socrates, of the marriage of practice and theory. I wanted to make you feel to what extent the vicissitudes of his life, the lessons it had sold him so dearly, those that he had learnt from wise men, all combined in his mind. The soul of this daring Phoenician never ceased from pondering upon the problem of navigation. Within himself, the Ocean was unceasingly astir. What can man pit against that inconstant universe, wrought upon from afar by the heavenly bodies, traversed by swelled surge and transparent mountains, uncertain at its shores, unknown in its depths; the origin of all that lives, but an impenetrable tomb with the motion of a cradle and a covering of light? —His busy daemon urged him on to make the best ships whose keel ever cut wave. And whereas his rivals remained content to imitate the models then in use, and in copy after copy continued building the bark of Ulysses, if not the immemorial ark of Jason, he, Tridon the Sidonian, ceasing not to fathom the unexplored regions of his art, breaking up the petrified combinations of ideas, and taking up things at their source . . .

Socrates

Most people in reasoning, dear Phaedrus, use notions that not only are "ready-made," but have actually been made by nobody. No one is responsible for them, and so they serve everyone badly.

Phaedrus

But he, as I tell you, had made for himself a clear insight all his own. . . .

Socrates

Insight of this kind can alone be universal. . . .

Phaedrus

He would passionately imagine the natures of the winds and the waters, the mobility and the resistance of their fluids. He would ponder upon the birth of tempests and calms, the circulation of warm currents, and of those immiscible streams which flow, mysteriously sure, between dark walls of salt water; he would consider the whims and veerings of the breezes, the uncertainties of sea floors and channels, and of treacherous estuaries. . . .

Socrates

And how, by the gods, out of all this did he make a ship?

Phaedrus

He thought that a ship should, in some sort, be created by the knowledge of the sea, and should almost be fashioned by the very wave itself! . . . But this knowledge consists, in truth, in replacing the sea, in our reasoning, by the actions that it exercises on a body—so that we have to discover the other actions which counterbalance those of the sea, and thus we have to deal only with an equilibrium of forces, both groups borrowed from nature, where they did not interact to any useful purpose. But our powers in this matter are limited to the disposing of forms and forces. Tridon used to tell me that he imagined his vessel hanging in one scale of a great balance, the other scale carrying a mass of water. . . . But I hardly know what he meant by that. . . . And then again, the restless sea does not remain satisfied with this equilibrium. All is complicated by movement. He sought therefore for the form a hull should have if the bottom was to remain more or less constant, whether the ship rolled from side to side—or danced in any other way about some center. . . . He would draw strange figures which for him made visible the secret properties of his float; but for my part I could see in them nothing in the least like a ship.

And at other times he would study the movement and the speed of craft; hoping and despairing in turn to imitate the perfection of the swiftest fishes. Those that swim easily on the surface, and play in the foam between their dives, interested him most of all. He would speak with the abundance of a poet of the tunnies and porpoises, amid whose leaps and gambols he had lived so long. He would sing their great bodies polished like weapons; their snouts that seem flattened by the mass of water that withstood their progress; their fins, as rigid and cutting as iron, but sensitive to their fishy thoughts, and steering towards their destinies as their whims dictate; and then their live mastery in the heart of storms! It was as though he himself felt their well-adapted forms conducting from head to tail, by the quickest way, the waters which lie in front of them, and which must be put behind them that they may advance. . . . It is an admirable thing, O Socrates, that on the one hand, if no obstacle impedes your progress, progress is quite impossible; all the efforts you make destroy one another, and you cannot push in one direction without pushing yourself away from the other with an equal force. But, on the other hand, once the necessary obstacle is present, it works against you; it drinks up your fatigues, parsimoniously metes out to you space in time. Here the delicate act of the artist intervenes in the choice of a form: for the form has to take from the obstacle what it requires in order to advance, but must only take what least checks the mover.

Socrates

But can one not copy the porpoise or the tunny themselves, and despoil nature directly?

Phaedrus

I thought so in my simplicity. Tridon undeceived me.

Socrates

But is not a porpoise a kind of ship?

Phaedrus

Everything changes with size. Form does not follow increase in size so simply; neither the solidity of materials, nor the directing organs, could endure it. If one quality of the thing increases according to arithmetical ratio, the others increase otherwise.

Socrates

Did Tridon at least turn out anything really good?

Phaedrus

Some marvels of seaworthiness. Some others, no doubt, are at the bottom, and, encrusted with barnacles, await the hour when the sea goes dry.

But I saw the purest of all his daughters, the spruce *Fraternity*, with her tapering lines, that evening she left on her first voyage. Her scarlet cheeks took all the kisses that leapt up to meet her on her course; the well-stretched triangles of her full, hard sails held down her quarter to the wave. . . .

Socrates

O Life! . . . And for me, the black, loose-flapping sails of the vessel with its load of priests, which as it labored back from Delos, dragging on its oars . . .

Phaedrus

How little you seem to relish living your beautiful life over again!

Socrates

Phaedrus, my pale Phaedrus, Brother Shade of my Shade, how infinite, I feel, would be my regrets if they had some substance to work on, and if flesh were not wanting for their exercise! They begin to stir, but it all comes to nothing! They are sketched out, but they cannot take on color! . . . Is there anything vainer than the shadow of a sage?

Phaedrus

A sage himself.

Socrates

Alas yes! a sage himself, who leaves behind him only the reputation of a talker, and various sayings abandoned to immortality. . . . What did I do but lead the rest of mortals to believe that I knew much more than they about the most doubtful things? —And the secret for getting it believed lies in a death so well conducted, adorned with such injustice, and surrounded with such friendships, that it darkens the sun, and disconcerts nature. What is more to be feared than the making of death a sort of masterpiece? . . . Life cannot defend herself against those undying death scenes. She invincibly imagines—in her simplicity—that the finest part of the tragedy begins after the last word of the last line! . . . Man's deepest glances are those that go out to the void. They converge beyond the All.

Alas! alas! I have made use of a truth and a sincerity much more deceitful than are myths and inspired sayings. I taught what I invented. . . . I got children upon the souls I seduced, and I delivered them skillfully.

Phaedrus

You are hard on all of us.

Socrates

If you had not listened to me, my pride would have sought some other way of subjugating your thoughts. . . . I should have built, sung. . . . O thoughtful waste of my days! What an artist I have destroyed! . . . What things have I scorned, and alas, what begotten! . . . I feel like the Judge of my own spiritual Netherworld pronouncing sentence against myself! Whilst the facility of my renowned sayings pursues and afflicts me, here am I raising up as Eumenides my actions that did not take place, my works that were never born—those glaring voids, vague and enormous crimes that they were: those murders, the victims of which are imperishable things! . . .

141

Phaedrus

Be comforted. . . . You would regret them much more if you had begotten them! Nothing seems so fair, nothing gnaws us with such bitter remorse as opportunities missed! But if we have let them go lost, is it not because we were unable to seize them without disturbing the whole course of the world?

Socrates

That is just what we should wish! . . . What soul would hesitate to turn the universe upside down in order to be a little more itself? You well know that we grant to all other things only the privilege of suiting us! —We wish quite precisely that the infinite Heavens and the earth and the sea and cities; and that men, too, and women more especially; and their souls, their energies, and their graces; and animals as well as plants—we even naïvely include the Gods—should all together, and each according to its beauty which complies with our desire, or according to that power which it brings to our weakness—be but the aliments, the ornaments, the condiments, the props, the resources, the lights, the slaves, the treasures, the ramparts, and the luxuries of our sole individual selves! As if our flame alone, and that so brief spell of absolute duration which is hers, were worthy to consume all that was, is, and shall be, in order that, in her, all delight and all knowledge may flash forth once for all, for the being which she animates and devours! . . . We believe that all things, that all the bounty of Time, are but a titbit for our palates, and we cannot think the contrary.

Phaedrus

You dazzle me and you fill me with dismay!

Socrates

You do not know what I now see I might have done!

Phaedrus

I confess that this shadow of despair that has come over you and these promptings of remorse which seem to be striving in your mien for the mastery, make of me a phantom of bewilderment. If the others were to hear you!

Socrates

Do you think that they would not understand?

Phaedrus

Nearly everybody here is vain enough about his past life. The very criminals make a parade of their abominable renown. Nobody wants to admit that he was mistaken; and you, Socrates, whose pure name still overawes even the envious ghosts, you would make them these sad confidences and ask for their pity and their scorn?

Socrates

Would that not be to go on being Socrates?

Phaedrus

You must not wish to begin again. . . . One never succeeds a second time. . . .

Socrates

Do not be yet more bitter.

Phaedrus

I must confess that your words have wounded my friendship a little. Surely you understand that if you lower yourself, and if you depreciate Socrates, then Phaedrus who gave himself up to him so piously, Phaedrus sees himself reduced to the last extreme of folly and blind simplicity!

Socrates

Alas! such is our condition! But I am trying to make something of it. Think you not that we ought now to employ this boundless leisure which death leaves us, in judging and rejudging ourselves unwearyingly, revising, correcting, attempting other answers to the events that took place, seeking, in fine, to defend ourselves by illusions against nonexistence, as the living do against their existence?

Phaedrus

And what is it you want to depict against this background of nothingness?

Socrates

The Anti-Socrates.

Phaedrus

I can imagine more than one. There are several contraries to Socrates.

Socrates

This one will be . . . the constructor.

Phaedrus

Good. The Anti-Phaedrus is listening to him.

Socrates

O coeternal with me in death, faultless friend, and diamond of sincerity, hear then:

144

It served no purpose, I fear, to seek this God, whom I have tried all my life to discover, by pursuing him through the realm of thought alone; by demanding him of that most variable and most ignoble sense of the just and the unjust, and by urging him to surrender to the solicitings of the most refined dialectic. The God that one so finds is but a word born of words, and returns to the word. For the reply we make to ourselves is assuredly never anything other than the question itself; and every question put by the mind to the mind is only, and can only be, a piece of simplicity. But on the contrary, it is in acts, and in the combination of acts, that we ought to find the most immediate feeling of the presence of the divine, and the best use for that part of our strength that is unnecessary for living, and seems to be reserved for the pursuits of an indefinable object that infinitely transcends us.

If, then, the universe is the effect of some act; that act itself, the effect of a Being, and of a need, a thought, a knowledge, and a power which belong to that Being; it is then only by an act that you can rejoin the grand design, and undertake the imitation of that which has made all things. And that is to put oneself in the most natural way in the very place of the God.

Now, of all acts the most complete is that of constructing. A work demands love, meditation, obedience to your finest thought, the invention of laws by your soul, and many other things that it draws miraculously from your own self, which did not suspect that it possessed them. This work proceeds from the most intimate center of your existence, and yet it is distinct from yourself. If it were endowed with thought, it would divine your existence, which yet it would never succeed in probing, nor in conceiving clearly. You would be for it a God. . . .

Let us now consider this great act of constructing. Note, Phaedrus, that when the Demiurge set about making the world, he grappled with the confusion of Chaos. All formlessness spread before him. Nor could he find a single handful of matter, in all this waste, that was not infinitely impure and composed of an infinity of substances.

He valiantly came to grips with this frightful mixture of dry and wet, of hard and soft, of light and gloom, that made up this chaos, whose disorder penetrated into its smallest parts. He disentangled that faintly luminous mud, of which not a single particle was pure, and wherein all energies were diluted, so that the past and the future, accident and substance, the lasting and the fleeting, propinquity and remoteness, motion and rest, the light and the heavy were as completely mingled as wine with water, when poured into one cup. Our men of science are always trying to bring their minds close to this state. . . . But the great Shaper acted in contrary wise. He was the enemy of similitudes and of those hidden identities that we delight to come upon. He organized inequality. Setting his hand to the rough matter of the world, he sorted out its atoms. He divided the hot from the cold, and the evening from the morning; he drove back almost all the fire into the subterranean hollows, and hung clusters of ice on the very trellises of dawn, beneath the vaultings of the eternal Ether. By him extension was distinguished from movement, night from day; and in his rage to disunite everything, he clove asunder the first animals, which he had just disassociated from the plants, into male and female. After he had finally disentangled even that which was most mixed up in the original confusion—matter and mind—he hoisted to the loftiest empyrean, to the inaccessible peak of History, those mysterious masses, whose silent irresistible descent into the uttermost depth of the abyss begets and measures Time. He squeezed out from the mud the sparkling seas and pure waters, lifting the mountains out of the waves, and portioning out in fair islands whatever concreteness remained. Thus he made all things; and, from a remnant of mud, humankind.

But the constructor whom I am now bringing to the fore finds before him, as his chaos and primitive matter, precisely that world order which the Demiurge wrung from the disorder of the beginning. Nature is formed, and the elements are separated; but something enjoins him to consider this work as unfinished, and as requiring to be rehandled and set in motion again for the more especial satisfaction of man. He takes as the starting point of his act, the very point where the god had left off. —In the beginning, he says to himself, there was what is: the mountains and forests; the deposits and veins; red clay, yellow sand, and the white stone which will give us lime. There were also the muscular arms of men, and the massive strength of buffaloes and oxen. But there were in addition the coffers and storerooms of intelligent tyrants and of citizens grown overrich by trade. And lastly there were priests who wished to house their god; and kings so puissant that they had nothing more to desire than a matchless tomb; and republics that dreamed of inexpugnable walls; and refined archons, who had such partiality for actors and fair musicians that they were all afire to build for them, out of the state treasuries, the most resonant theaters.

Now the gods must not remain without a roof, nor souls without drama. The masses of marble should not remain lifeless within the earth, constituting a solid night; nor the cedars and cypresses rest content to come to their end by flame or by rot, when they can be changed into fragrant beams and dazzling furniture. But still less should the gold of rich men lazily sleep its heavy sleep in the urns and gloom of treasuries. This so weighty metal, when it becomes the associate of a fancy, assumes the most active virtues of the mind. It has her restless nature. Its essence is to vanish. It changes into all things, without being itself changed. It raises blocks of stone, pierces mountains, diverts rivers, opens the gates of fortresses and the most secret hearts; it enchains men; it dresses, it undresses women with an almost miraculous promptitude. It is truly the most abstract agent that exists, next to thought. But thought exchanges and envelops images only, whereas gold incites and promotes the transmutations of all real things into one another; itself remaining incorruptible, and passing untainted through all hands.

Gold, limbs, projects, various substances, all are present; yet nothing results.

Here I am, says the Constructor, I am the act. You are the matter, you are the force, you are the desire; but you are separate. An unknown industry has isolated and prepared you according to its means. The Demiurge was pursuing his own designs, which do not concern his creatures. The converse of this must come to pass. He was not concerned about the troubles that were bound to spring from that very separation which he diverted or perhaps bored himself with making. He has given you the means of living, and even of enjoying many things, but not generally those which you particularly want.

But I come after him. I am he who conceives what you desire a trifle more exactly than you do yourselves; I shall consume your treasures with a little more consistency and genius than you consume them; and without a doubt I shall cost you very dear; but in the end everyone will have gained. I shall make mistakes sometimes, and we shall have some ruins; but one can always very profitably look upon a work that has failed as a step which brings us nearer to the most beautiful.

Phaedrus

It is fortunate for them that you are a dead architect!

Socrates

Must I be silent, Phaedrus? —So you will never know what temples, what theaters, I should have conceived in the pure Socratic style! . . . I was going to give you an idea how I should have carried out my work. I should first have set out all the problems, evolving a flawless method. Where? —For what? —For whom? —To what end? —Of what size? —And exercising an ever stricter control over my mind, at the highest point I should have realized the operation of transforming a quarry and a forest into an edifice, into splendid equilibriums! . . . And I was drawing up my plan with an eye to the purpose of the humans who pay me; taking into account localities, lights, shadows, and winds; choosing the site according to its size, its aspect, its approaches, the adjacent lands, and the true nature of the subsoil. . . .

Then out of raw materials I was going to put together my structures entirely ordained for the life and joy of the rosy race of men. . . . Objects most precious for the body, delightful to the soul, and such as Time itself must find so hard and so difficult to digest that he will be able to subdue them only by the assaults of centuries; and that only after having clothed them in a second beauty: a mellow gold upon them, a sacred majesty upon them, and, wrought by the flight of time, a charm which comes of comparisons growing up about them and of a secret tenderness that wraps them all about. . . . But you shall learn no more. You can conceive only the old Socrates, and your stubborn shade . . .

Phaedrus

Call it rather faithful, Socrates, faithful.

Socrates

In that case it must follow me; and change if I change!

Phaedrus

But do you mean to revoke in eternity all those sayings that made you immortal?

Socrates

Immortal there—relatively to mortals! . . . But here. . . . But . . . there is no *here*, and all that we have been saying is as much a natural sport of the silence of these nether regions as the fantasy of some rhetorician of the other world who has used us as puppets!

Phaedrus

It is in this that immortality rigorously consists.

DIALOGUE OF THE TREE

Gentlemen,

A certain circumstance—a chance, since chance is the fashion—having brought me back a while ago to Virgil's Eclogues (which I had not looked at, I confess, for many years), this return to school inspired me to write, like a school exercise, this fancy in the form of a pastoral dialogue some of which I shall read out to you. Speeches, more or less poetical, devoted to the glory of a Tree, are exchanged between a Tityrus and a Lucretius, whose names I have taken without consulting them.

P. V.

Lucretius

What are you doing here, Tityrus, lover of the shade, at ease beneath this beech, your gaze lost in the gold of the leaf-woven air?

Tityrus

I live, I wait. My flute is set between my fingers, and I make myself like this admirable hour. I would be the instrument of the general favor of things. I abandon to the earth the whole weight of my body: my eyes live up there, in the palpitating mass of light. Look how the TREE above us seems to revel in the divine ardor from which it shelters me: its desireful being, which is certainly feminine in essence, begs me to sing to it its name and give musical form to the breeze which passes through and gently harasses it. I await my soul. To wait is of great price, Lucretius. I shall feel the pure act of my lips as it comes, and all that I still ignore of myself, lover of the Beech, will quiver. O Lucretius, is it not a miracle that a shepherd, a man forgetting a flock, can pour out to the skies the fleeting form and as it were the naked idea of the Tree and of the instant?

Lucretius

There is no miracle, Tityrus, no prodigy which the mind, if it wills it so, cannot reduce to its own artless mystery. . . . I myself think your tree, and possess it in my own way.

Tityrus

But *you* profess to understand things: you dream you know much more about this beech than it could know itself if it had a thought which induced it to believe it could grasp itself. . . . *I* only wish to know my happy moments. Today my soul is making itself into a tree. Yesterday I felt it to be a spring. Tomorrow? . . . Shall I rise with the smoke from an altar, or soar above the plains, with the sense of power of the vulture on its slow wings—how do I know?

Lucretius

You are nothing then but metamorphoses, Tityrus. . . .

Tityrus

It is for you to say. I leave profundity to you. But since this mass of shade draws you, like an island of coolness in the midst of the fire of the day, pause and cull the instant. Let us share this good, and let us exchange between us your knowledge of this Tree and the love and praise it inspires in me. . . . I love thee, mighty Tree—I am mad about thy limbs. There is no flower, no woman, that moves me more than thou, great Being with manifold arms, or draws a tenderer fury from my heart. . . . Thou know'st it well, my Tree, that I come to embrace thee from the moment of dawn: I kiss with my own lips thy smooth and bitter bark; I feel myself the child of this our very earth. On the lowest of thy branches I hang my belt and my sack. From out thy tufted shade suddenly a great bird noisily takes flight, escaping from thy leaves, itself afraid, affrighting me. But the squirrel, without fear, runs down and scurries towards me: it comes to recognize me. Tenderly sunrise is born, and all things declare themselves. Each says its name, for fire of the new day awakens it in its turn. The nascent wind resounds high up among thy branches. It places there a spring: I note the lively air. But Thee it is I hear. O utterance confused, O language all astir, I would fuse all thy voices together! A hundred thousand moved leaves make what the dreamer whispers to the powers of dream. I reply to thee, my Tree, I speak to thee and tell thee my secret thoughts. All of my truth I tell, all of my rustic vows: thou know'st the all of me, the artless torments too of the most simple life, the life closest to thee. I look about to see if we are indeed alone, and I confide to thee what I am. Now I confess myself as hating Galatea; now when a memory drives me to rave aloud, I hold thee for her being, am turned into a transport, wishing madly to feign, and join and catch and bite something more than a dream: something that lives. . . . But at other times I make thee God. O idol that thou art—to thee, O Beech, I pray. Why not? There are so many gods in our countryside. Some of them so ugly. But thou, when the wind falls and the majesty of the Sun calms, crushes, and illumines all that is in space, thou bearest upon thy spreading limbs, upon thy numberless leaves, the burning weight of midday's mystery; time all asleep in thee endures only in the provoking buzz of the vast insect world. . . . Then thou appear'st to me a temple as it were, and no suffering or joy comes to me that I do not dedicate to thy sublime simplicity.

Lucretius

O virtuosity! Most wonderfully stirred! I listen and admire. . . .

Tityrus

No. That you cannot do. You smile about my Tree and dream about your own. My flute for you is but a plaything

of the breeze, when from a mortal's lips the breeze derives
its flight: it ripples through the instant, entertains the ear.
What is it for the soul—so potent and profound? It is scarce
more than a suspected fragrance. My voice pursues but the
shadow of a thought. But great Lucretius, you—you with
your secret thirst—what is the *word*, O what, when it
begins to sing? It loses in that act the power to follow
truth. . . . Yes, I know well the worth of what the Tree
imparts. It tells me what it would that I should wish to feel.
I change that which I love into yet further joys, abandoning
to air what comes to me from Heaven. Nothing more,
nothing less. . . . Ah no, I do not hope my pleasure should
exhaust anything else but me, all simple as I am. But you,
your brow weighed down by shadows which you form, in
the hope of a flash that should strike down the gods, you
make yourself all mind, and sealed against the light, your
eyes seek in yourself the being of what is. What to the day
appears, your reason rates as naught, and what our tree is
stammering to the light wind, the gentle quivering of its
stirred summit, its branches spreading wide—one ample
hesitance—and all its winged folk warbling without a
thought: what matters it all to you? You seek the Nature
of Things. . . .

Lucretius

This great Tree is for you only your fantasy. You think
you love it, Tityrus, but only see your charming fancy there,
which you bedeck with leaves. You love only your hymn—
and so please me the more. From the majestic Beech you
take wherewith to sing the eddies of its form and its sonorous
birds, its shade which welcomes you from the burning heart
of day, and, by the Muses blest, you duly celebrate upon
your fragile reed the mighty giant's charms.

Tityrus

Well, sing, yourself, in turn; to nature give decrees, to the vast earth, to bulls, to rocks, and to the sea; give to the wave its law, give to the flowers their form! Think for the universe, a monster without head, which, for itself, in man searches for reason's dream; but O do not disdain your simple listener. Open to him the wealth of truth's obscurities. What little of this beech do you know more than we?

Lucretius

Look, to begin with, well at this brute force, the powerful timber of these outstretched limbs: look at the solid matter life has made, fitted to bear the weight of northern blast and to stand firm against the cataract; the waters of the dense maternal earth, drawn from the depths for years on end, at last bring this hard substance to the light of day. . . .

Tityrus

Substance as hard as stone, and fit like it to carve.

Lucretius

Ending in branches, too, which end in leaves themselves, and then at last the mast which, fleeing far and wide, will scatter life abroad. . . .

Tityrus

I see what you would say.

Lucretius

See then in this great being here a kind of river.

Tityrus

A river?

157

Lucretius

A river all alive whose sources downward plunge and in the earth's dark mass find the pathways of their mysterious thirst. It is a hydra, O Tityrus, at grips with the rock, growing and dividing to embrace it the better; a hydra, which, becoming ever finer, impelled by the damp, dishevels into a thousand hairs so as to drink up the least presence of water that impregnates the massive night wherein are dissolved all things that have lived. There is no hideous beast of the sea more greedy and multiple than this tousle of roots, blindly certain in their progress towards the depths and dampnesses of the earth. But their advance proceeds, irresistible, with a slowness which makes it implacable as time. Into the empire of the dead, of the mole and the worm, the toil of the tree inserts the powers of a strange subterranean will.

Tityrus

What marvels, O Lucretius, you recount! . . . But shall I tell you what I think of as I listen? This treacherous tree of yours which into the deep shade insinuates its live substance through a thousand strands, and which draws up the juice of the deep-dormant earth, recalls to me . . .

Lucretius

Well, what?

Tityrus

It recalls love.

Lucretius

Why not? Into your human sense, towards your shepherd's soul, what I say penetrates and finds its echo there. Thus has my utterance, Tityrus, touched the point, the deepest knot of being, where unity resides—whence radiates through us, illumining the world with one sole thought, all the most secret store of its similitudes. . . .

Tityrus

I know not. . . . What you say is dark to me, O Lucretius.

Lucretius

Enough that I understand myself. But you, speak freely—of love, too, if you wish. Yet rather sing to me that metamorphosis. . . . How came it in your mind that a growing plant could make you dream of love, that need of pleasure? Sing.

Tityrus

Pleasure? O love is not of such a simple substance.

Lucretius

What could you wish it more than universal urge? What is it but a goad fashioned by destiny?

Tityrus

A goad! . . . And mine you say is but a shepherd's soul! . . . A goad! . . . You make of love a cowherd's tool, no more? The love that you conceive is but the love of rams and wild things of the woods. These brutes, in sudden fits, all drunken with their seed, endeavor hideously, when in the heat of rut, to give their flesh release from this live poison. They love, but without love, as chance encounter bids. A shepherd knows it well, who plays his part at times, composing at his will the female and the male, whenever he would have the kidlings of his choice.

Lucretius

And so—see destiny traversed by Tityrus! . . . Into the dark where fate fumbles you thrust your hands. . . . You cheat. . . .

Tityrus

And is that not the business of men, whose total sum of wit is used to torment nature, trammel up their lives, and even would baffle death?

Lucretius

Do not get lost beneath my abstract trellises. Just leave the aphorisms and reasonings to me. I'm waiting for the tree and love, which you would join. Sing to me, if you will, something your very own. Whilst to your songs my ear lends itself willingly, I fear I'll not be won by your philosophy.

Tityrus

Well, listen then. This is what comes to me:

> *Unless love grow to the utmost it is naught:*
> *Growth is its law; it dies from being same,*
> *And dies in one who dieth not of love.*
> *Living upon a never quenchèd thirst,*
> *Tree in the soul whose living roots are flesh*
> *Who lives from living in the quick of life*
> *It lives from all, from bitter as from sweet,*
> *And from the cruel better than the kind.*
> *Great Tree of Love who ceaseth not to bind*
> *And build into my weakness strangest powers,*
> *A thousand moments which the heart embowers*
> *For thee are foliage and shafts of light!*

But whilst thy rapture opening into flowers
In the gold sun of happiness appears,
Thy selfsame thirst, whose depth grows with the hours,
Deep in the shade, draws from the spring of tears. . . .

Lucretius

These are no verses, are they? There's a riddle here.

Tityrus

I was improvising. 'T was but the first essay of a poem to be. What you a moment back said to me of this Tree made me dream Love. Yes, Love together with the Tree can in our minds unite into one sole idea. The one and the other are something which, born of an imperceptible germ, grows ever larger and ever stronger, spreads and branches forth; but so far as it rises towards heaven (or happiness) just so much must it down descend into the dark substance of that which we unknowingly are.

Lucretius

Our earth? . . .

Tityrus

Yes. . . . And it is there, in the depths of the shades wherein melt and are mingled what there is of our human kind, and what there is of our living substance, and what there is of our memories, and of our hidden strengths and weaknesses, and finally that which is the shapeless sense of not having always been and of having to cease to be, that there is to be found what I called the "spring of tears": THE INEFFABLE. For our tears, I hold, are the expression of our powerlessness to *express*—that is, by words to rid ourselves of the oppression of what we are. . . .

Lucretius

You go far for a shepherd. Do you then always weep?

Tityrus

Yes, I can always weep. And, shepherd though I be, I have observed that there is no thought which, pursued as close as may be to the soul, does not lead us on to those wordless shores, those silent shores where alone subsist pity, tenderness, and the kind of bitterness inspired in us by that mixture of the eternal, the fortuitous, and the ephemeral: which is our lot.

Lucretius

And so that is what you meditate upon when you spend your summer nights keeping watch over your sleeping flock, whilst a whole herd of stars, goaded hither and thither upon the horizon, by the silent flash of lightning, or traversed by the unforeseen flight of meteors, seems to browse on time, and—as a herd or flock step by step crops its way—crops the future endlessly?

Tityrus

What am I to do? At that nocturnal hour, the Tree appears to think. It is a being of shade. The birds, all now asleep, leave it alone alive. It quivers to its depths: as speaking to itself. For fear inhabits it, as she inhabits us, when we are all alone at midnight with ourselves, and quite delivered up a prey to our own truth.

Lucretius

Most true indeed: for we have only ourselves to fear. The gods and destinies cannot work aught in us but by the treachery of our all-sensitive fibers. Over our lower souls they hold a coward's sway; the power they wield is not the act of Wisdom's self; divinity just finds in bodies that are weak, for final argument, the torture of the sage.

Tityrus

But is not fire the very end of the Tree? When its being becomes one mass of racking pain, it writhes; but changes itself to light and ashes pure, rather than molder, rotted by stagnant water, nibbled by vermin. . . .

Lucretius

Tityrus, if you can, choose from among these ills! Better not think on them; for what could be more useless? For ills, when ills there are, stand out clearly enough. . . . But if I were to you the comrade of your nights, both of us in the shade unseen at the Tree's foot, reduced to our two voices, to a single being, evenly crushed by the burden of so many stars, I should recount to you, sing to you what my inner contemplation of the Idea of the Plant sings and says to me.

Tityrus

I should listen to you devoutly in the night; I should lose the feeling of my ignorance; I should not understand everything that you said, but I should so love it, with so great a desire that it should be true, with such a rapture of spirit, that I can conceive no surer happiness, no more incorruptible moment. . . .

Lucretius

The being filled with wonder is lovely, like a flower.

Tityrus

Forgive me: I could not refrain from interrupting you as you were speaking of that Idea of the Plant. . . .

Lucretius

Do you not see that every plant is a *work* and that there
is no work without an idea?

Tityrus

But I see no author. . . .

Lucretius

The author is but a detail, useless more or less.

Tityrus

You overwhelm me. . . . You make sport of Tityrus! . . .
But I am a reasonable animal, and I know just like you that
all things need their cause. All that exists was made; all
supposes someone, man or divinity, a cause or a desire, some
potency to act. . . .

Lucretius

Are you quite sure nothing can be by itself, causeless and
reasonless, without preceding end?

Tityrus

Quite sure.

Lucretius

And do you sometimes dream?

Tityrus

Yes, before every dawn.

Lucretius

Just as the dawning day acts on the granite of the illustrious statue, making it resound, so Memnon-Tityrus im-

provises at dawn in himself, for himself, the most astounding tales. . . . But your dreams, Tityrus, are they of any worth? Do you on waking know that they were worth the dreaming?

Tityrus

There are such lovely ones. . . . Some too that are so true! . . . Some that are all-divine. . . . And others, sinister. . . . So strange they sometimes are that they seem formed to be dreamed by some other sleeper, as though they mistook the absent, and mixed defenseless souls in the night. . . . And there are cruel ones for having been too sweet: such and such bliss is rent just as it fills me, abandons me to the day upon the shores of truth. . . . My flesh is still all quivering with love, but the spirit holds back and coldly contemplates the dying palpitation of its body. . . . And the two ends of the cut reptile writhe . . . apart.

Lucretius

And so you simply were an onlooker constrained to undergo the spectacle. But who, tell me, who is the author of this drama?

Tityrus

The author. . . . I know none. I can find nobody.

Lucretius

You?

Tityrus

Assuredly not I, for these strange games of sleep cannot be played unless I be shut out from their preparing: no terrors otherwise, nor surprises, nor charms.

Lucretius

There is no author, then. You see it, Tityrus: a work
without an author is not impossible. No poet organized
these phantasms for you, and you would never from yourself have drawn delights like these nor those abysses of your
dreams. . . . No author. . . . There are then things which
create themselves, without a cause, and so make their own
destiny. . . . That is why I reject, as being a childish need of
mortal minds, the simple-minded logic which seeks to see in
all an artist and his aim, both distinct from the work. Man—
innocent before everything that he sees, upon the earth, or
in the skies, the stars, beasts, seasons, the semblances of rules,
of happy foresight or of harmony—questions: "Who made
this? Who willed it?" Thinking he must compare everything with those simple objects which our hands produce:
our vessels, tools, abodes, arms—all those compounds of
matter and spirit which our needs engender. . . .

Tityrus

Do you think you yourself can better grasp the nature of
things?

Lucretius

I try to imitate the indivisible mode. . . . O Tityrus,
I think that in our substance is to be found without going
too deep that identical potency which in like manner produces all life. All that the soul puts forth is very nature's
self. . . .

Tityrus

What, you think everything which comes to us essential?

Lucretius

Not everything that comes to us, but the coming itself. . . . I tell you, Tityrus, between all that's alive there is

a bond, is a similitude, which can engender hatred quite as much as love. The like caresses or devours its like. Whether he eat a lamb or cover a she-wolf, the wolf can do no more than make or remake wolf.

Tityrus

But could you yourself make or remake Tree?

Lucretius

I have told you that I feel, born and growing in me, a Plantlike virtue, and I can merge myself in the thirst to exist of the hard-striving seed, moving towards an infinite number of other seeds throughout a plant's whole life. . . .

Tityrus

Let me stop you. . . . A question comes to me.

Lucretius

What I was going to tell (perhaps to sing) to you would have, I think, dried up the spring of words which suddenly wells up from the depths of your mind. But speak! . . . If I asked you to wait, you would inwardly—and self-contentedly—listen to yourself instead of listening to me. . . .

Tityrus

Yes, do you not think, O Wise Man that you are, that our knowledge of anything whatsoever is imperfect if it is confined to the exact notion of that thing, if it is limited to the truth, and if—having succeeded in changing the naïve view into a clear idea, the pure outcome of investigation, experiment, and all the formal observances which eliminate error or illusion—it remains satisfied with that perfection?

167

Lucretius

What more do you need than what is? And is not the true the natural frontier of the intelligence?

Tityrus

I certainly think, for my part, that reality, always infinitely more rich than the true, comprises, on every subject and in every matter, the quantity of misunderstandings, of myths, of childish stories and beliefs which the minds of men necessarily produce.

Lucretius

And you do not wish this weed to be burned by the wise men, exhaling an odor agreeable to Minerva?

Tityrus

If you transplant it, tending it well apart, it ceases to be weed; some use can be found for it. But in my ignorance and my simplicity, here's what I have to say. Once we hold the true firmly, and no longer fear to get lost in vain whims, wisdom should retrace her steps, take up again and gather as things human all that was created, forged, thought, dreamt, and believed, all those prodigious products of this our mind, those magic and monstrous stories that spring so spontaneously from us. . . .

Lucretius

It is certain (and indeed strange) that the true can be known to us only by the use of many artifices. Nothing is less natural!

Tityrus

I have noticed that there is not a thing in the world that has not been adorned with dreams, held for a sign, explained by some miracle, and this all the more as the concern with knowing the origins and first circumstances is more naïvely potent. And that is doubtless why a philosopher whose name I have forgotten coined the maxim: IN THE BEGINNING WAS THE FABLE.

Lucretius

Was it not I who said it? But I have said so many things that this one is as much mine as not. . . .

Tityrus

You are so rich! . . . But I return to my discourse, and by it to our TREE. . . . Do you know the *Marvelous History of the Infinite Tree*?

Lucretius

No.

Tityrus

And about the cedar tree charged with love? Nothing? In the island of Xiphos? . . .

Lucretius

I know nothing about the cedar—nothing of the island.

Tityrus

And the most astounding?

Lucretius

I know nothing about the most astounding.

Tityrus

The most astounding history of Trees is surely that of those giant apple trees, the fruit of one of which offered to whoever bit its fabulous flesh an eternal life, whilst the fruit of the other, no sooner tasted, produced a strange clearness in the mind of the eater: he felt invaded by a shame attached to the things of love. A sudden redness enveloped his whole being, and he felt his nakedness as a crime and a branding. . . .

Lucretius

What strange combinations find themselves at ease together in your memory, Tityrus!

Tityrus

I love what astonishes me and only retain that which would excite but forgetfulness in the mind of a wise man.

Lucretius

And the infinite tree?

Tityrus

In the first age it was, when virgin was the earth, and man still to be born, and all the animals. The Plant was master and covered the whole face of the soil. It might have remained the sole and sovereign form of life, offering to the eyes of the gods the varied splendor of the seasons' colors. Motionless by nature of each of its individuals, it moved about in the form of species, mastering extension bit by bit. It was by the number of its seeds (which it scattered madly to the winds) that it advanced and spread in the manner of a conflagration devouring all it finds to devour; and that is what, without man and his labors, grasses and bushes would still be doing. But what we see is nothing compared with the power of conquest by leaps and bounds of winged seeds, in that heroic age of vegetable vigor. Now (hear this, Lucretius) it happened that one of those seeds, whether through the excellence of the ground into which it fell, or through the favor of the sun upon it, or through some other circumstance, grew like no other, and from a grass grew into a tree, and that tree into a prodigy! Yes! It seems as though a sort of thought and will took form in it. It was the greatest and most beautiful being under the sky, when, divining perhaps that its tree life was only tied up with its growth and that it only lived because it grew larger, there came upon it a sort of overweening and arborescent madness. . . .

Lucretius

By which this tree was a sort of mind. What's loftiest in the mind can only live through growth.

Tityrus

As an athlete, his legs set wide apart, brings his effort to bear upon the columns between which he is placed and pushes them none the less energetically with his arms distended by willing, so that tree became the focus of the most powerful urge and the most tense form of force that life has ever produced, an enormous force, though insensible at any instant, capable of gradually lifting a rock as big as a hill or of overturning the wall of a citadel. It is said that at the end of a thousand centuries, it covered with its shadow the whole of immense Asia. . . .

Lucretius

What mortal sway that shadow must have held! . . .

Tityrus

Yes, that imperial Tree made night beneath itself. No ray of sun could pierce its foliage, within whose denseness all the winds got lost, whilst its brow shook off hostile storms, as massive oxen flick away the gnats. The rivers were no more, such was the sap it drew from sky and earth at once. Rearing in the dry azure its tense solitude, it was the God Tree. . . .

Lucretius

A marvelous adventure, Tityrus!

Tityrus

Forgive me. I have thrust this story innocently athwart the deeper, wiser discourse which you were going to make me on our present theme.

Lucretius

I know not if I can speak better than a Fable. . . . I wished to speak to you of the feeling I sometimes have of being Plant myself, a Plant that thinks, but does not distinguish between its diverse potencies, nor its form from its force, its port from its place. Forces, forms, size, and volume, and duration are but a single river of existence, a tide whose liquid expires in hard solidity, whilst the dim will of growth rises and bursts, and would again become will—in the light and innumerable form of seeds. And I feel myself live the un-heard-of enterprise of the Type of the Plant, invading space, improvising a dream of branches, plunging into the midst of the mire, and drinking in the heady salts of the earth, whilst in the free air it opens by degrees to the bounty of the sky, green thousands of lips. . . . As much it goes down deep, so much it rises up: it chains the shapeless, it attacks the void; it struggles that it may change all into itself, for that is its Idea! . . . O Tityrus, it seems to me I am sharing with my whole being in that meditation—powerful, active, and rigorously followed up in its design—which the Plant bids me make. . . .

Tityrus

You say the Plant meditates?

Lucretius

I say that if someone on earth does meditate, it is the Plant.

Tityrus

Meditate? . . . Perhaps the meaning of this word is obscure to me?

Lucretius

Do not trouble about that. The lack of but one word makes a phrase live the better: its opening is the vaster—it proposes to the mind to be mind a little more and so fill in the gap.

Tityrus

I am not clever enough. . . . I cannot conceive that a plant should meditate.

Lucretius

Shepherd, what you perceive of a shrub or a tree is only the outside and instant, offered up to the indifferent eye, which only skims the surface of the world. But to spiritual eyes the plant presents not just a simple object of humble, passive life, but a strange will to join in universal weaving.

Tityrus

A shepherd's all I am—spare him, Lucretius!

Lucretius

Is not to meditate to deepen oneself in Order? Just see how the blind Tree with its diverging limbs grows up about itself, faithful to Symmetry. Life in it calculates; it raises up a structure; and radiates its rhythm through branches and their twigs, and every twig its leaf, even at the very points marked by the nascent future. . . .

Tityrus

Alas, how can I follow?

Lucretius

Do not fear, listen only: when to your soul there comes the shadow of a song, a desire to create which takes you by the throat, do you not feel your voice swell to become pure sound? Do you not feel them melt—both its life and your vow—towards the sound desired, whose wave wafts you along? Ah! Tityrus, a plant is a song whose rhythm deploys a definite form and within space displays a mystery of time. Each day it raises up a little higher the burden of its twisted scaffoldings, and offers thousandfold its leaves to the sun, each one delirious at its station in air, according to what comes of breeze to it and as it believes its inspiration unique and divine. . . .

Tityrus

But you become yourself a very tree of words. . . .

Lucretius

Yes. . . . Radiant meditation fills me with rapture. . . . And in my soul I feel all words atremble.

Tityrus

I leave you in that admirable state. But I must now gather my flock again. Mind the cool of the evening—it comes so quickly.

APPENDIX

EDITOR'S NOTE

THOUGH not in the form of a dialogue, "Paradox on the Architect" has certain thematic and other relations to the works in this volume, especially to *Eupalinos* and *Dialogue of the Tree*. It is one of the earliest expressions of Valéry's preoccupation with architecture, which played so strong a part in forming his imagination. While announcing some of his own serious and persistent themes, this piece of youthful prose is a tissue of the notions and mannerisms common to young poets at the time: the obsession with "music," with Wagner, with the aesthetic mysticism of "correspondences" and of "analogies" between the arts, of which Orpheus was the frequent symbol. In 1891, when this prose poem first appeared, Valéry was only nineteen; he had not yet visited Paris, but a year earlier he had met Pierre Louÿs and André Gide at Montpellier. It is to them the "Paradox" is dedicated, under the pseudonyms Claude Moreau and Bernard Durval.

The French text is included here for its rarity and special interest. One curious feature of this small work is its combination of verse and prose, a technique which Valéry used more fully later on in *Dialogue of the Tree*. The closing lines in French actually form a rhymed sonnet.

PARADOXE
SUR L'ARCHITECTE

à MM. Claude Moreau et Bernard Durval

Il naîtra, peut-être, pour élever les premiers tabernacles et les sanctuaires imprévus où le Credo futur, à travers l'encens, retentira.

Il rachètera l'Art superbe épuisé par trois cents années d'injurieuses bâtisses, et tant de lignes inanimées! ..

Autrefois, aux siècles orphiques, l'esprit soufflait sur le marbre; les murailles antiques ont vécu comme des hommes, et les architectures perpétuaient les songes. En d'autres temps, le faste mystique des cathédrales éternisait l'âme pieuse des nations: les pinacles érigés attestaient la ferveur des villes, et l'horreur des éternels supplices éveillait dans le grès tourmenté d'épouvantables bestiaires. La basilique était l'antiphone de pierre, et les hautes nefs priaient éternellement ... Puis, c'est le silence et la décadence; l'architecture agonise dans les Académies. Les floraisons merveilleuses se dessèchent, et, tristement s'éteignent les yeux lucides de jadis, les vitraux et les roses chimériques.

Maintenant, c'est une jeunesse, c'est la frêle et la délicieuse enfance que l'art traverse une fois de plus. Ce siècle mourant fut la longue et la laborieuse nuit d'amour, nuit de peine où la gloire nouvelle fut conçue. Voici l'aurore et la blanche Épiphanie! Nous, comme les rois fabuleux, saluons la divine naissance!

Seule, l'architecture veuve n'est pas encore dans la joie. Tous les autres arts sont serrés autour des hautaines enseignes d'or. Les purs artistes ont trouvé dans l'adoration indistincte des musiques, des couleurs et des mots, une grâce mystérieuse qui touche leurs œuvres particuliers. Et le rêve de chacun se

PARADOX ON THE
ARCHITECT

To MM. Claude Moreau and Bernard Durval

He will be born, perhaps, to raise the first tabernacles and unpredicted sanctuaries, wherein will resound, through the incense, the Credo of the future.

He will redeem that superb Art exhausted by three hundred years of offensive building and so many inanimate lines! . . .

Formerly, in the Orphic Ages, a spirit was breathed upon the marble, the walls of antiquity lived as men do, and the works of architecture gave perpetuity to dreams. At other times, the mystical splendor of the cathedrals gave an eternal character to the piety of nations: the pinnacles that were raised testified to the fervor of cities, and the horror of eternal punishments called dreadful bestiaries to life in the tortured sandstone. The basilica was the antiphon of stone, and the lofty naves were an eternal prayer. . . . Then there is silence and decadence; architecture dies a slow death in the Academies. The marvelous blossoms wither, and sadly grow dim and die the lucid eyes of former times, the wondrous stained-glass and rose windows.

Now, art is once again passing through a period of youth—its frail and delicious childhood. Our dying century was the long and laborious night of love, a night of toil wherein the new glory was conceived. See now the dawn and the white Epiphany! Like the fabulous kings let us hail the divine birth!

Widowed architecture alone has not yet shared in the new joy. All the other arts have rallied round the lofty standards of gold. Pure artists have found in the indistinct adoration of music, colors, and words a mysterious grace which touches

magnifie et s'exalte, et tout cet univers exaspéré qu'abritent les esprits magnifiques, où flambent les fleurs et les métaux, où les êtres sont plus beaux et plus douloureux, s'enferme, —ô triomphe des luttes avec l'Ange!—dans une parole, dans l'hymen délicat des nuances, dans la vie personnelle et décisive des sons! Les mondes immenses, dont les Têtes prédestinées sont les habitacles d'élection, apparaissent, résumés en de secrètes suggestions, sous chacune des formes objectives que leur impose la native préférence des créateurs.

Ainsi, l'effort du siècle a conquis l'intelligence des principes futurs. L'analyse esthétique d'aujourd'hui a prévu la victorieuse synthèse des prochaines œuvres. Mais, encore, la lourdeur maussade des attiques traditionnels, la morne roideur des fermes d'acier ne s'émeut pas au contact de tant de vie! Loin du petit bataillon sacré qui invective la laideur et le lucre, et qui chante l'hymne sous les flèches, loin des vers, loin des symphonies, les maçons élaborent des combinaisons incurieuses. La poésie a obtenu son constructeur de Temples qui taillait les mots longuement comme des pierres dures; mais aucun architecte n'a su être Flaubert . . .

Demain, le suprême édificateur surgira d'un peuple, si ce peuple et le temps n'en sont pas les meurtriers. Sa pensée sera forte et harmonieuse, car il aura bu le lait d'une Déesse.

Ce soir, je veux en ces lignes vaines que dicte le caprice avec la songerie, prévoir l'invisible étoile,—cette âme lointaine et par mon âme désirée.

Je la devine musicienne, et longtemps recluse dans la pure solitude de son rêve.

D'abord, elle aura puisé l'exacte harmonie et les magiques infinis où les rythmes aboutissent, dans les ondes frissonnantes et profondes que les grands symphonistes ont épandues, Beethoven ou Wagner. Car de subtiles analogies unissent

the particular works of each. And the dream of each is magnified and exalted, and that whole exasperated universe sheltered by magnificent minds, wherein flowers and metals blaze, and beings are more beautiful and suffer more, is enshrined—O triumph of wrestling with the angel!—in a single word, in shades delicately wed, in the personal and decisive life of sounds! The immense worlds, of which predestinate Heads are the elected abodes, appear, summed up in secret suggestions, under each of the objective forms imposed upon them by the inborn preferences of their creators.

Thus the effort of the age has comprised in its conquering grasp the principles of the future. The aesthetic analysis of today has anticipated the victorious synthesis of the works soon to be. But as yet the sullen heaviness of traditional attic stories, the dismal rigidity of steel cross-girders, remain unstirred at the contact with so much life! Far from the sacred little band which reviles ugliness and lucre, and which sings its hymn beneath the arrows—far from verses, far from symphonies—masons toil at combinations that lack all invention. Poetry has obtained her builder of Temples, who chiseled and chiseled his words as though they were hard stones; but no architect has known how to be Flaubert. . . .

Tomorrow the supreme constructor will arise in the midst of a people, if that people and Time are not his murderers. His thought will be strong and harmonious, for he will have drunk the milk of a Goddess.

This evening I would wish, in these vain lines, dictated by caprice and reverie together, to forecast the invisible star —that distant soul by my own soul desired.

I divine that soul as a musician's, long cloistered in the pure solitude of its dream.

And first: it will have drawn the exact harmony and infinite enchantments in which rhythms culminate, from the

l'irréelle et fugitive édification des sons, à l'art solide, par qui des formes imaginaires sont immobilisées au soleil, dans le porphyre. Le héros, qu'il combine des octaves ou des perspectives, conçoit en dehors du monde . . . Il assemble et féconde ce qui n'existe ni ailleurs, ni avant lui, et se plaît souvent à rejeter le souvenir précis de la nature. Dans l'immortelle nuit où l'idée, jaillissante comme une eau vive, se livrera vierge à l'architecte de l'Avenir, quand, libre des choses visibles et des types exprimés, il aura trouvé le symbole et la synthèse de l'Univers intérieur qui confusément l'inquiétait, lors cette volonté et cette pensée de musique agrandie composera sa création originale comme une haute symphonie—aussi indépendant des apparences, aussi abstrait de la réalité directe, aussi détaché du Passé et des prochains phénomènes et des liens de sa mémoire matérielle qu'un Edgar Poë en ces étranges poèmes où tout de cette vie est oublié!—Ainsi, se manifestera l'indicible correspondance, l'intime infinité qu'il faut discerner, sous des voiles habituels et mensongers, entre deux incarnations de l'art, entre la façade royale de Reims, et telle page de Tannhauser, entre l'antique magnificence d'un grand temple héroïque et tel suprême andante brûlant de flammes glorieuses!

Un jour, le palais, le sanctuaire érigera les lueurs de ses frontons inconnus, proclamant l'âme vibrante et résonnante de l'artiste. Lui, n'aura fait que pétrifier et fixer dans la durable ordonnance des matériaux la clarté céleste et les ombres émues dont les mesures et les accords des orchestres auront confié l'immense spectacle à son cœur! Toute sa pensée sera reflétée dans l'œuvre, et sur la façade miraculeuse il y aura des tristesses reposées et de brillants sourires.

Mélancolies et sourires et charmes insaisissables, le créateur s'en sera abreuvé dans les fleuves spirituels dont nous avons parlé.

deep, quivering waves poured forth by the great symphonists, Beethoven or Wagner. For subtle analogies unite the unreal and fugitive edification of sounds to the solid art by whose means imaginary forms are immobilized in the sun, in porphyry. The hero, whether he combine octaves or perspectives, conceives outside the world. . . . He assembles and fecundates that which exists neither elsewhere nor before him, and often takes pleasure in rejecting the precise memory of nature. In the immortal night in which the virgin idea, springing like live water, surrenders itself to the architect of the Future, when, free from things visible and types expressed, he has found the symbol and synthesis of the Inner Universe which obscurely troubled him—then that will and thought of a larger music will compose his original creation like a lofty symphony—as independently of appearances, as abstracted from direct reality, as detached from the Past and from proximate phenomena and from the bonds of his material memory as an Edgar Poe in those strange poems where everything of this life is forgotten!—And thus will become manifest the ineffable correspondence, the intimate infinity which must be discerned, under the veils of custom and deceit, between two incarnations of art, between the royal façade of Reims and some page of *Tannhäuser*, between the ancient magnificence of a great heroic temple and some supreme andante, gloriously aflame!

One day the palace, the sanctuary, will raise the gleam of its unknown pediments, proclaiming the sounding, vibrant soul of the artist. He will have done no more than petrify and fix in the durable order of his materials the celestial clarity and those poignant shades whose immense spectacle the rhythms and harmonies of orchestras have confided to his heart! His whole thought will be reflected in the work, and

Car les cuivres sont resplendissants comme des portes d'or, et les cordes étirées sur les violons versent avec une tendresse sacrée l'ineffable lumière de vitrail qui aime les cœurs merveilleux des ciboires; car les orgues liturgiques creusent pour le rêve des coupoles dans des saphirs et d'énormes dômes pleins de tonnerre; mais les flûtes s'élancent comme de graciles colonnettes, si hautes qu'un vertige les couronne; et d'autres instruments et les voix humaines semblent scintiller afin d'illuminer le chœur balsamique et nocturne où l'Être souffrant et triomphant officie pour la déplorable foule!

Telles sont les magnificences latentes sous les mélodiques formes, telles sont les richesses ouvertes à celui qui aura l'intelligence mathématique des plus lointains rapports, qui saura dégager les lignes, discerner les courbes, évoquer les couleurs significatives que renferme une symphonie, et qu'expriment les instruments dociles à de grands artistes.

Enfin, de par cette volonté sortira de terre le monument tangible et visible, projeté dans la matière après avoir ébloui le pays mystérieux où les anges l'avaient édifié avec de saintes harmonies!

Et voici dans l'air bleu le Décor tel un somptueux désir d'enfant réalisé . . .

Voici comme un prélude annonciateur des rites, l'archivolte s'ouvrir avec des promesses, et les nervures légères incurver leurs gestes adoucis, et les jeunes grâces des arcs jaillir en des inclinaisons féminines de tiges. Par les verrières, des mauves et d'obliques lilas sur les dalles tombent, et pleuvent des pluies longues de pierreries.

Et c'est la forêt du silence . . . Là, les hautes efflorations des piliers et les colonnes liliales, croissent dans l'ombre fastueuse parmi le rare pavement,—elles qui sont fleuries de

upon the miraculous façade will be sadnesses at rest and radiant smiles.

Melancholies and smiles and elusive charms—the creator will have drunk them in from the spiritual streams we have spoken of.

For the brasses are resplendent like gates of gold, and strings stretched upon violins pour out with a sacred tenderness the ineffable stained-glass light that loves the wondrous heart of the pyx; for the liturgical organ hollows out, for dream, cupolas in sapphire and vast domes full of thunder; but the flutes shoot up like slender little columns—set so high that dizziness crowns them; and other instruments and human voices seem to scintillate so as to illumine the balsamic, nocturnal choir, where the suffering and triumphant Being officiates for the lamentable crowd!

Such are the magnificencies latent beneath the melodic forms, such are the riches open to him who will have the mathematical understanding of the most remote relationships, who will be able to bring out the lines, discern the curves, evoke the significant colors which a symphony encloses, and which those instruments express that are docile to great artists.

And then, in virtue of that will, there will issue from earth the tangible and visible monument, projected in matter, after having dazzled the mysterious country where angels had built it out of sacred harmonies!

And lo! in the blue air the Structure—like the realization of some sumptuous desire of a child . . .

See, like a prelude announcing rites, the archivolt opening with promises, and the light nervures curving inward their softened gestures, and the young grace of the arches springing in a feminine inclination of stems. Through the stained win-

fleurs mystérieuses, et qui portent sculptés sous leurs abaques, comme des fruits de l'Arbre de la science, les universels, les magiques symboles.

Et c'est la forêt où l'on oublie, où l'on écoute! Le long des parois précieuses, coupées par les hiératiques bandeaux, des lotus nimbés d'or, inattendus et purs, épanouissent leurs pâles calices, cueillis peut-être au fond de wagnériennes rêveries, dans les plaines de la lune et traduits en gemmes fondues sur les murailles du sanctuaire.

Un largo triomphal et total éclate enfin sous l'ultime voûte; de tous les motifs exprimés se dégage et s'essore le secret, le glorieux amour absolu . . .

Or, celui qui entre et qui regarde, ébloui de l'œuvre tirée d'un songe, retrouve inévitablement d'héroïques souvenances.

Il évoque, en un bois thessalien, Orphée, sous les myrtes; et le soir antique descend. Le bois sacré s'emplit lentement de lumière, et le dieu tient la lyre entre ses doigts d'argent. Le dieu chante, et, selon le rythme tout-puissant, s'élèvent au soleil les fabuleuses pierres, et l'on voit grandir vers l'azur incandescent, les murs d'or harmonieux d'un sanctuaire.

Il chante! assis au bord du ciel splendide, Orphée! Son œuvre se revêt d'un vespéral trophée, et sa lyre divine enchante les porphyres, car le temple érigé par ce musicien unit la sûreté des rythmes anciens, à l'âme immense du grand hymne sur la lyre! . . .

dows, mauves and oblique lilacs upon the flagstones fall, and down rain long showers of gems.

And it is the forest of silence. . . . There, the lofty blossomings of the pillars and the lily-columns grow in the gorgeous shade amid the rare pavement—blossomings that flower with mysterious flowers, and that bear, carved beneath their abacus, like fruits of the Tree of Knowledge, the universal, the magic symbols.

And it is the forest where one forgets, where one listens! Along the precious walls, intersected by the hieratic fillets, gold-haloed lotuses, unexpected and pure, open wide their pale chalices, plucked perhaps from the deeps of Wagnerian reverie, in the plains of the moon and translated into molten gems upon the walls of the sanctuary.

A triumphal and total largo bursts forth at last beneath the ultimate vault; from all the motifs expressed there emerges and soars the secret, the glorious absolute love. . . .

And to him who enters and looks, dazzled by the work drawn from a dream, inevitably there come heroic memories.

In a Thessalian wood he evokes Orpheus, beneath the myrtles; and the ancient night descends. The sacred wood is slowly filled with radiance, and the god holds the lyre between his silver fingers. The god sings, and, obedient to the all-powerful rhythm, there soar into the sun the legendary stones, and growing toward the incandescent azure, lo! harmonious rise a sanctuary's golden walls.

He sings, Orpheus, enthroned against the splendid sky! And see, a vesperal trophy crowns his work; his lyre, divinely struck, enchants the porphyries; for the temple which this musician raises now unites the certitude that springs from ancient rhythms with the vast soul of the great hymn upon the lyre! . . .

NOTES

I. BIBLIOGRAPHICAL NOTES

ALL of Valéry's formal dialogues are here collected for the first time.

The French titles of the works in this volume are:

> *Socrate et son médecin*
> *Orgueil pour orgueil*
> *Colloque dans un être*
> *L'Ame et la danse*
> *Eupalinos ou l'architecte*
> *Dialogue de l'arbre*
> *Paradoxe sur l'architecte*

The first three originally appeared together in the second, trade edition of *Mélange* (Paris: Gallimard, 1941). They were not included in the original, limited edition of *Mélange* published for Les Bibliophiles de l'Automobile-Club de France (Paris, 1939).

The two major dialogues were first published separately, but almost at the same moment: *Eupalinos ou l'architecte* in the first and only number of *Architectures* (September, 1921), although two fragments, with the subtitle *Dialogue des morts*, had been published in *La Nouvelle Revue française* (March, 1921); *L'Ame et la danse* in *La Revue musicale* (December 1, 1921). They were later brought together in one volume,

Eupalinos ou l'architecte, précédé de L'Ame et la danse (Paris: N. R. F., 1923).

Dialogue de l'arbre appeared first in a volume with photographs by Laure Albin-Guillot, under the title *Arbres* (Bordeaux: Rousseau Frères, 1943); there was an offprint of the dialogue alone, under its full title, in the same edition. Valéry read the work before the annual joint session of the Cinq Académies, October 25, 1943; it was accordingly published by the Institut de France (1943), with a short introduction written for the former occasion (translation, p. 152). It was later included in the volume *Eupalinos, L'Ame et la danse, Dialogue de l'arbre* (Paris: N. R. F., 1944).

Paradoxe sur l'architecte, a piece of Valéry's earliest published prose, appeared in the review *L'Ermitage* (March, 1891) and was republished in *Œuvres,* Vol. A (Paris: Sagittaire, 1931). The text of 1931 is reproduced here; it is identical with the earlier text, except for the omission of some italics and a footnote citing three lines of Mallarmé's sonnet on Wagner. The last two paragraphs form a sonnet, with a missing rhyme in the first line. Published by Pierre Louÿs as a poem, *Orphée,* in his review *La Conque* (May, 1891), it was revised by Valéry for the second edition of his *Album de vers anciens* (Maestricht: Stols, 1926), where only three lines of the original survive.

Three of these works have been translated into English before: *Eupalinos, or the Architect* by William McCausland Stewart (Oxford University Press, 1932), revised for the present edition; *Dance and the Soul* by Dorothy Bussy (London: John Lehmann, 1951); and "Colloquy within a Being" by William Jay Smith (*New Mexico Quarterly,* spring, 1955).

II. TEXTUAL NOTES

The Prefaces

WALLACE STEVENS wrote his prefaces to *Eupalinos* and *Dance and the Soul* in the winter and spring of 1955. They are, "except, perhaps, for a poem or two," says his literary executor Samuel French Morse, "Stevens's last significant work." The edition of Valéry's *Collected Works* thus elicited from the American poet his final response to a mind with whom he clearly had much in common.

The quoted texts were translated by William McCausland Stewart.

ix. *Gloire du long désir, Idées:* "Glory of long desire, Ideas"; a line from Mallarmé's poem, *Prose: pour des Esseintes.* See p. 77.

Denis Saurat refers to Eupalinos: cf. his *Modern French Literature* (New York: Putnam, 1946), pp. 159–60.

x. *Letter to Paul Souday: Lettres à quelques-uns* (Paris: Gallimard, 1952), p. 147.

xi. *Letter to Dontenville:* ibid., pp. 214–15.

xx. *Jean Wahl might have diminished this:* see his *Poésie, pensée, perception* (Paris: Calmann-Lévy, 1948), p. 88.

Alain says: cf. his *Propos de littérature* (Paris: Paul Hartmann, 1934), p. 30.

xxi. *It was natural for such pages to give Rilke pleasure:* see Rainer Maria Rilke, *Letters,* tr. Jane Bannard Greene and M. D. Herter Norton (New York: Norton, 1945, 1948), II, pp. 279–80, 366.

xxii. *Chose légère, ailée, sacrée:* "A light and winged and sacred thing"; Plato's description of the poet, *Ion* 534B. Wallace Stevens took the phrase from Louis Séchan, *La Danse grecque antique* (Paris: De Boccard, 1930), where he found it used as a motto, and cited in the text, p. 12. See herein, p. xxvi.

xxii. *I thank you greatly for your attention: Lettres à quelques-uns,* pp. 189–91.

xxviii. *To explain a thing is to deform it:* André Levinson, *Paul Valéry, philosophe de la danse* (Paris: La Tour d'Ivoire, 1927), p. 11.

The Dialogues

The translations in this volume were made by William McCausland Stewart, Professor of French Language and Literature at the University of Bristol. He knew Paul Valéry and discussed with him a number of difficult points in the translation of *Eupalinos*. Likewise with Rainer Maria Rilke, its German translator. In April, 1955, Wallace Stevens wrote, in a letter to this editor: "Nothing could please me more than to know that you are making use of a translation of the dialogues by William Stewart. This man's translation of the *Eupalinos* is a beautiful thing."

In both the very early *Paradoxe sur l'architecte* and the very late *Dialogue de l'arbre,* Valéry combined verse and prose: the former work ends in a sonnet; the latter contains concealed alexandrines and decasyllables that rise at one point to a song in rhymed verse. The translator has used a similar technique in his version of both these works.

17. *The dawn unveiled to me the whole of hostile day:* "L'Aube me dévoilait tout le jour ennemi"; a line from Valéry's *La Jeune Parque.*

21. *Intelligenti pauca:* "Few words to the knowing."

22. *I rush to the waves to re-emerge alive:* Valéry is here playing a variation on *"Courons à l'onde en rejaillir vivant,"* a line from his *Le Cimetiére marin.*

63. πρὸς χάριν: "For pleasure"; "for beauty."

77. *Gloire du long désir, Idées:* see note for p. ix.

The very admirable Stephanos: Stéphane Mallarmé; see Prefaces, p. xv.

152. Concerning this introduction, see the bibliographical note on the *Dialogue de l'arbre,* p. 192.

169. *In the Beginning was the Fable:* Valéry himself is the philosopher; he used this phrase at the end of his essay on Poe's *Eureka,* and elsewhere.

This colophon was chosen from a number of drawings by Paul Valéry of his favorite device.